MANKIND, NATION AND INDIVIDUAL

*from a Linguistic
Point of View*

by the same author

ESSENTIALS OF ENGLISH GRAMMAR
PHILOSOPHY OF GRAMMAR
LANGUAGE
HOW TO TEACH A FOREIGN LANGUAGE
CHAPTERS ON ENGLISH
MODERN ENGLISH GRAMMAR
    (Six volumes)
NOVIAL LEXIKE
A SYSTEM OF GRAMMAR
LINGUISTICA

MANKIND, NATION AND INDIVIDUAL

INDIVIDUAL

*From a Linguistic
Point of View*

BY

OTTO JESPERSEN

LONDON
GEORGE ALLEN & UNWIN LTD
MUSEUM STREET

FIRST PUBLISHED IN GREAT BRITAIN IN 1946

MADE AND PRINTED IN GREAT BRITAIN
BY CHARLES AND READ
27 CHANCERY LANE, LONDON, W.C.

CONTENTS

Chapter   Page

  I. Speech and Language 1
  II. Influence of the Individual 27
 III. Dialect and Common Language 38
 IV. Dialect and Common Language (concluded) 61
  V. Standards of Correctness 84
 VI. Correct and Good Language 123
 VII. The Stratification of Language 141
VIII. Slang 149
 IX. Mysticism of Language 166
  X. Other Eccentricities of Language 186
 XI. Conclusion Universal Human Elements 204

CHAPTER I

SPEECH AND LANGUAGE

I have undertaken to speak of Language in its relation to Mankind at large, to the Nation and to the
Individual. There is no doubt or ambiguity as to the
meaning of Mankind or the meaning of the Individual;
but the term Nation is by no means so clearly defined. It has never been settled what is to be understood by a Nation. Many will say that the Swiss
form a Nation in spite of the fact that they speak
three, or indeed four, different languages. On the
other hand it is maintained that Great Britain and the
United States are two distinct nations in spite of their
having a single language. As early as the middle of
the nineteenth century people began to speak of a
Canadian nationality or an Australian nationality on
the ground that the inhabitants of these lands in spite
of their linguistic and political ties to the mother-
country were beginning to feel themselves in some
way different from Englishmen at home. Portuguese
and Brazilians, Spaniards and Argentines are also illus-
trations of the fact that something more than a com-

mon language goes to make a Nation. There are many factors in the process. Geographical unity and a common history play their rôles by the side of — sometimes in defiance of — language, so that it is impossible to define 'Nation' in a way that will suit all cases and satisfy everybody. This, however, does not concern us in our present study, which deals with language exclusively, so that we can lightly dismiss from consideration all the political, military and emotional sides of nationality, though they have shown themselves — and not least in the last two centuries — to be as potentially dangerous as dynamite. Accordingly when in the present course of lectures a Nation is spoken of as that which is intermediate between Mankind at large and the Individual, you must understand by 'Nation' merely a linguistic unit, a linguistic community.

What I mean by the title I have chosen is as follows. Each one of us is first and foremost — in his language as well as in other things — an Individual with a stamp of his own —, of this or of that sex, of a particular age, with particular features of mind and body: after this, he is an Englishman or a Dane or a Frenchman or whatever he is by Nation: and finally he belongs to Mankind at large. Or we can reverse the order and say that first and foremost he is a Man, in the second place he has the stamp of a particular Nation; in the third place, as against his fellow-countrymen, he is Himself. This is the complicated game which we have set ourselves to disentangle, so far as concerns Language and linguistic activity.

It is a familiar experience that the first time one encounters people of the Yellow Race, they look all alike: on nearer acquaintance one notices the difference between Chinamen, Japanese and Siamese; and finally in each of these national groups one detects the individuals. It is the same with languages. The Danish song says, 'If you can talk all languages, they are all the same thing to you'. But it is still truer to say that if people can talk no language but their own, all foreign languages are the same thing to them: they sound so far alike, that they are all frightful gibberish, 'barbarian' as the Greeks called it. It is only later that one gets to hear and feel the differences between one foreign language and another. Then, when, either at school or later in life, we begin to *learn* a foreign tongue, it presents itself to us as a unit: 'In French 'a horse' is *'cheval'*, and 'I give' is 'je donne':' that means that *all* Frenchmen speak so. The French Grammar and the French Dictionary make no distinction between one Frenchman and another, but tar them all with the same brush. But the deeper we penetrate into the foreign language, the more we discover the little differences — at first covered under the great agreement in essentials — differences of style in the different authors one reads, shades of difference in the pronunciation of the different people one hears speak, — just such as we are familiar with in our own language where differences are detected at once. 'Every bird', says the proverb, 'has its own song', but the proverb is meant mainly to apply to the difference between particular kinds of birds — the nightingale's rhapsody is not like the caw of the crow or the lark's trill. The proverb takes no account of the further fact that one nightingale's warblings give a different melody from those of another, and that every sparrow of a surety knows his nearest friends by their voices just as we know ours.

Lévy-Bruhl quotes a famous maxim of Auguste Comte's: 'il ne faut pas définir l'humanité par l'homme, mais, au contraire, l'homme par l'humanité.' To me, so far at least as language is concerned, the truth seems to be that one must neither define 'mankind' by 'man' nor 'man' by 'mankind', but must constantly strive to understand the individual by help of the whole and the whole by help of the individual (or rather, of individuals); the particular man is only what he is, and his language is only what it is, in virtue of his life in the community, and the community only exists in and in virtue of the particular beings who together constitute it.

The most notable advance that has been made in the theoretical conception of the nature of language since the serious study of language first began consists in this, that we no longer do what was so frequently done in earlier times, that is, conceive language as a self-existent thing or substance, or — to use an expression frequently employed — as an organism, that lives and dies like a plant or any other organism, but have learnt to see that language in its essence is a human activity, an effort on the part of one individual to be understood by, or at least come into relation with, another individual. Along with this and in consequence of this we have come to lay stress on the individual as the factor which at any moment produces, or may produce, words and sentences: and the recognition of this has helped us to understand many phenomena of language, both as regards its state at a given period and its changes from one period to another; or to use learned terms, both synchronistic and diachronistic, or, as I should prefer to say, both static and dynamic (or kinetic): or more simply, as the objects of description and of historical treatment.

We shall never approach a complete understanding of the nature of language, so long as we confine our attention to its intellectual function as a means of communicating thought. But this one-sidedness is to be seen in highly distinguished investigators. Hermann Paul in his admirable Rectorial Address on *Völkerpsychologie* (München 1910) [1] says of the purpose of language: 'its original function is always however to serve as a means of imparting something.' No, neither its original function nor its present-day function. As to the origin of language, in my *Progress in Language*, and more recently in the final section of my book *Language*, I have tried to show that we only begin to divine what the origin of language was when after tracing back its history as far as we can, we see that the earliest language was anything but intellectual, that it was indeed a sort of half-way house between singing and speech with long almost meaningless conglomerations of sounds, which served rather as an outlet for intense feelings than for an intelligible expression of them, and which in any case was not primarily thought of as a means of telling other people something or other, though by a roundabout way it did come eventually to serve as a means of communication.

However, I shall not here concern myself with the

[1] Printed in *Süddeutsche Monatshefte*.

question what language was at its very beginning, but shall consider exclusively what language is at present for living people.

We may first call to mind three competing statements, first the everyday remark that language exists to express one's thoughts, next Talleyrand's well-known *mot* that language exists to hide one's thoughts, and lastly Søren Kierkegaard's improvement of it, that language is used by many people to hide the fact that they have no thoughts. How a language may spring up with the express purpose, not exactly of hiding thoughts, but at least of hiding the communication of them, so that it is not understood by those who hear the words unless they are among the initiated, will be treated in a later lecture in which I shall speak of thieves' language and other languages of concealment. Here I shall speak of language in its more normal forms.

That logicians should attach chief or even exclusive importance to the employment of language as a means of expressing thought, is what one might expect. So Jevons 1 says that language serves three ends: 1. As a means of communication. 2. As a mechanical aid to thought. 3. As an instrument of record and reference. He does not see that the last use is only a subordinate branch of the first, for when one makes a note of something to refer to afterwards and so calls to mind one's previous thoughts, this does not differ essentially from the first end of language — to communicate one's thoughts to another person. One is oneself and another person at the same time when one reads one's own past notes.

¹ *Elementary Lessons of Logic.* 287.

As to Jevons's second end, 'as a mechanical aid to thought', it is indeed certain that the possession of a language does very essentially aid one's thoughts. On the other hand it must not be forgotten that some of the deepest thinkers have frequently complained that the traditional language had been in some cases a hindrance to them in thinking a thing out to the very bottom. With its fixed vocabulary and forms of sentence it had forced the thought on to a beaten track, so that they had been compelled to follow old lines and had come to think very much as other people had thought before.

However that may be, I can certainly not follow Jevons when he says: 'In its first origin language was used chiefly, if not exclusively, for the first purpose', or in his setting up of these three intellectual ends as the only ends for which language is employed. They apply only, one might say, to men and women who think, and to them only in their most academical moments.

Let us now by way of contrast hear what a highly gifted woman says of the purpose of language. Mme de Staël[1] is speaking of the French language: 'elle n'est pas seulement comme ailleurs un moyen de communiquer ses idées, ses sentiments et ses affaires, mais un instrument dont on aime à jouer et qui ranime les esprits comme la musique chez quelques peuples et les liqueurs fortes chez quelques autres.' That is admirable! The only fault I have to find is that she speaks as if this function of language were something only to be found in France. It is

[1] Quoted by Gerber, *Sprache als Kunst*, I. 79.

quite possible that in France it is found in a higher degree and practised with greater art than in most places, but I am still disposed to believe that Mme de Staël has proclaimed a universal truth. There are people everywhere who are equally capable of being intoxicated with their language and revelling in the enjoyment of their own voices, or who at any rate do not wait to open their lips till they have something to say which is worth hearing. In what I have written about the language of children, I have pointed out that children would never learn to talk at all if they were surrounded exclusively by thinkers who only used language as a means of communicating thought. Luckily for them in their earliest years they have the chance of hearing those about them, especially mother and nurse and other women, talk on end with everlasting repetitions even when they are absolutely certain that the dear baby does not understand a syllable of what they say. Notice again how people who are fond of animals will talk at length to their dog or cat or horse. We shall have a later opportunity of drawing attention to all that meaningless jingle which in more or less metrical form makes up a great deal of what men say or sing. We must then never forget that the organs of speech besides serving for the conveyance of thought, and before they begin to be used for that purpose, are one of mankind's most treasured toys, and that not only children but also grown people, in civilized as well as in savage communities, find amusement in letting their vocal chords and tongue and lips play all sorts of games.

So we arrive at the social side of Speech. The same thing holds. In social intercourse words for the most part are not uttered to report something or impart something or to explain matters of fact or the like, hardly even to express a common feeling, but to gratify the craving for sociability.[1] This side of the matter has recently been emphasized by the Polish ethnographer Bronislaw Malinowski in a supplement which he has written to a stimulating book by the two English psychologists, C. K. Ogden and I. A. Richards, *The Meaning of Meaning* (London, 1923).

Malinowski got into this way of thinking when he was living among the natives of the Trobriand Islands near New Guinea and observed how such primitive races behaved in regard to the use of language. According to Malinowski, language in its primitive forms may be seen and studied with human activities as background, and may be regarded as one of the ways in which men behave themselves in given practical situations. The main thing is that by means of speech the one person comes in contact with the other. All human beings are impelled to seek the society of others, to feel themselves in intercourse with them: and that is where language helps. To man in the state of nature there is little that is more uncomfortable than another man's silence. The man that says nothing is a disquieting and uncanny creature. The stranger who cannot speak your language is with all savage races a natural enemy. With savages — even with many people among the lower classes in our communities — silence is not only a sign of unfriendliness, but may easily become an insult and be considered a

[1] 'On parle souvent devant l'interlocuteur, plutôt que pour lui personne n'écoute.' Delacroix L. P. 308.

mark of bad character. A word or two by way of greeting, a mere 'Good day!' or a careless remark about the weather, or the 'where do you come from?' of the Melanesian islanders [1] — think also of such a sentence as 'What, are you here?' which clearly is not said to convey anything or inquire about anything — all utterances of this kind have really no other purpose than to bring about contact between man and man, a pleasant connexion, which is the first approach to the friendly relation which is sealed by a meal enjoyed in common: they help one to get over the uncomfortable tension one feels when one finds oneself with a stranger and not a word is spoken.

Even when in a primitive community incidents are reported by help of language, we have not to do primarily with a communication of thought, but with the sociable relation which the reporter brings about by his words. And even where there is this intercourse by word of mouth, the words alone do not tell the whole tale — the context, the circumstances, the whole situation and relation between the two interlocutors, aid the understanding of the story. Malinowski is right in laying stress on this and sharply drawing our attention to the difference between an oral communication of this kind and the texts in literary works and inscriptions with which philologists have especially to occupy themselves, and in which the writer's intention was to convey some tidings to the knowledge of posterity without external assistance. But he is wrong in believing that philologists have solely occupied them-

[1] I may add that a peasant in Jutland in the same way begins every conversation with a stranger with: 'Hur æ han fræ?'

selves with texts of this kind and that it is only ethnologists who have noticed those phases of the life of language which he has spoken of: there is indeed a living philology which stands opposed to the older school that chiefly occupied itself with dead civilizations. But even philologists of this more modern type may be glad to have these views set forth as well and as clearly as has been done by Malinowski, and at the same time to have it brought home to them that by children (and largely by grown people) language is employed not so much to formulate and express thoughts, as to give vent to feelings, and especially to have their wishes gratified, that is, rather to bring about some action on the part of others, than to describe actions, still less, express thoughts. So to the primitive consciousness of the savage as well as of the child, the Word comes to possess a force, a power, serving to effect certain results. But I shall speak later of this magical power of words and the superstitious belief in its efficacy.

*

If we would get a clear view of the nature of Language, we must at the very beginning take stock of a distinction made with great acuteness by the brilliant French-Swiss philologist Ferdinand de Saussure, and accepted since, with some change, by his pupil Charles Bally, and very recently by the English phonetician, Harold E. Palmer. Mr. Palmer was summoned to Japan by the Japanese Government to organize linguistic teaching, and in the course of considering the best method of teaching English to Japanese students, hit upon the same distinction which had been made by Saussure.

The two things to be kept apart are called by Saussure 'langue' and 'parole'; by Palmer 'language' and 'speech'. A certain difficulty arises from the distinction made in French between 'lángue', used of a particular language, and 'langage', of language in the abstract.[1]

How does Saussure define his two main concepts 'parole' (speech) and 'langue' (language)? According to him, Speech is the individual thing, the action of an individual ('un acte individuel de volonté et d'intelligence'): the individual is always master of it. Language on the contrary is the sum of the word-pictures which are stored in the mind of all individuals with the same values. Language is not a function of the man who speaks, but exists only in the mass. It is therefore the social side of the matter, something which the individual must take as he finds it, which he can neither make nor alter. It exists only in virtue of a sort of agreement arrived at between the members of the linguistic community (p. 32) Saussure's expression reminds one of Rousseau's 'social contract'. Accordingly, he tells us, a language can be fixed: by help of a dictionary and a grammar one can give a tolerable representation of it. It is also possible to study the language apart from the speech: we no

---

[1] De Saussure, *Cours de Linguistique générale,* Lausanne et Paris, 1916. Harold Palmer, *Memorandum on Problems of English Teaching,* Tokyo 1924. Cp. also many passages in H. Delacroix, *Le Langage et la Pensée,* Paris 1924, especially 48 ff.; and A. Sommerfelt, *Bull. Soc. Ling.* 25, 25 (1924): 'La langue est le type d'un fait social. Elle est une partie du langage: elle est indépendante de l'individu qui la parle, mais d'autre part, existe seulement là où il y a des individus. Nous ne pouvons pas la changer à notre gré.'

longer speak t ie dead languages, but we can very well 'nous assimiler leur organisme linguistique'. In another place (p. 233) he speaks of new-formations according to analogy, and says that at first they belong only to speech, as being the chance creation of a single individual. It is in that sphere, that is to say, on the borderline of language ('en marge de la langue') that one first gets the phenomenen. Cp. p. 237: 'Nothing comes into the language without having been first tried in speech'. Accordingly the task set to linguistic science ('la linguistique) is the study of the language, while, by comparison with this, speech is for philologists something accidental and secondary or subordinate.

Charles Bally [1] is disposed to hold to Saussure's distinction in the main, but he considers that Saussure has laid too much weight on language as something purely intellectual, as an outcome of collective wisdom, while he himself would lay stress on the emotional element, 'le langage affectif. According to him, there is a constant struggle going on between the speech of individuals and the organized language which never satisfies the whole body 'The organized, normal, intellectual language' satisfies the craving for the communication and understanding of thoughts: 'speech' on the contrary stands at the service of actual life; what it would express is feeling, desire, action: the creations of 'speech are for the most part emotional and subjective.' In the regular siege-war which 'speech' makes upon language, the former always succeeds in getting a few soldiers admitted into the fortress.

[1] F. de Saussure et l'état actuel des etudes linguistiques, Geneve 1913.

It is certain enough that the emotional element plays a great part in the evolution of language, and no less certain that this has often been overlooked by philologists, but when Bally lays so much stress on language, in contrast to speech, having an essentially intellectual character, I can only suppose that his argument is based on the current French grammar as learnt in French-speaking schools. This is indeed logical to a degree, and this sort of teaching perhaps explains a good deal in the Frenchman's sharp distinction between 'la langue', on which so much stress is laid at school, the conventional, normalized, regular language, and on the other hand 'la parole', representing the unchecked tendencies of a free life.

In Palmer we find nearly the same distinction that we found in the Swiss philologists. He says (p. 40): That heterogeneous and complex subject vaguely alluded to under the general term 'language' is in reality two different and incommensurable subjects. First we have (A) the sum of the mental and physical activities involved when one person communicates to another (by gesture, articulation or by written signs) any given concept (i. e. thought, notion or emotion). This Palmer calls speech. Next we have (B) the sum of the conventions adopted and systematized by a socialized mass of users of A in order to ensure common intelligibility : this is language. A, then, is a set of personal activities, whereas B is a set of conventions, a code. A commercial code is not the same thing as the acts involved when transmitting a message by such a code; the code of Marine Signals is not the same thing as the acts involved in hoisting the flags; the musical code of notes and rests is not the same thing as the acts performed by the musician; the code represented by a Railway Time Table is not the same thing as the acts performed by one who travels by train. In short, an act (or activity) is not the same thing as the code in accordance with which it is executed. The two thing are not identical with practice and theory, for we have the theory and practice of Speech, and the theory and practice of Language. The theory of speech is studied by psychologists, the practice of speech is manifested by the child in the nursery or by the pupils of the successful teacher of a foreign speech. The theory of language is studied by writers on the science of language; the practice of language is manifested by those who are engaged in teaching or studying the codes themselves. Each time we are successful in communicating our concepts we are practising Speech; each time we successfully analyze a mode of expression, paraphrase it or build up a foreign sentence by purely synthetic methods, we are practising Language. [But isn't a successful analysis 'theory'? and if through building up a foreign sentence in the way indicated we successfully communicate our concepts, isn't that speech-practice? The fourfold distinction is not very clear.]

When we ask what value we shall attach to the distinction between Speech and Language made by the three authors, my impression is that they have got hold of a truth but have unmistakeably run it to extremes, and that it will be well for us to bring things into their right relation.

In Saussure's dictum quoted above about analogy-formations which must first show themselves in 'la parole', and only after being tried there can enter 'la langue', there is really nothing (if we strip it of the stilted terms) but a statement that everything must be first used by a particular person before it can be generally recognized — nothing therefore but what is really extraordinarily obvious, nay, *banal*. 'La parole' is the product of a single man, 'la langue' the product of the community. But the community consists solely of individuals, and nothing in the language — any more than in other things — becomes the possession of the community, so long as it is only found with a single person or some few. In the distinction drawn between 'Speech' and 'Language', I can see nothing but a sort of transformation of the theory of a 'folk-mind' or 'collective mind' or 'herd-mind', as opposed to and exalted above the individual mind, a theory which is found in various German investigators and one which Hermann Paul among others very rightly combated. [1] Mind and consciousness are found only in the individual, and even if all, or nearly all, individuals in a community think the same, and feel the same with regard to this or that, or are accustomed to react in a like manner to this or that situation, we still do no. get a 'folk-mind' which behaves like this, but many minds which resemble one another. The name 'Folk-psychology' 'Psychology of the People' hides a great deal of fundamental confusion of mind and ought to be dismissed once and for all, with its offspring 'Mass-psychology', and perhaps also 'National Mentality' which has become a fashionable term since the War. The last term may indeed be employed if one is re-

[1] Especially in his Rectorial Address mentioned above.

solute in using it only of an agreement which has come about from natural causes, between a number of individual minds. A mystically assumed 'common mind' really explains nothing whatever in any department of life, any more than the assumption of a mystical 'common-stomach' would serve to explain how it is that people react in like manner to foods and poisons.

Certainly neither Saussure nor his successors talk of a 'folk-mind' or 'folk-spirit' in the same way as Steinthal and Wundt, but it is a step in the same direction when it is said that Language as opposed to Speech only exists in the mass, that is, in the folk, in the nation, the linguistic community. And they seem even to be getting near to a still more erroneous conception, that which I above designated the conception of an elder generation which ought by now to have been vanquished, I mean the conception that a Language has an independent existence like some sort of substance or organism. Are we not reminded of that idea when it is said that Language (as opposed to Speech) can be represented in a dictionary and a grammar, or classed with a telegraphic code or a railway time-table? The truth lies on the contrary in Saussure's remark that Language is the sum of the word-pictures that are stored in the soul of all the individuals. But then we see also that this is nothing else than the necessary fundament of the speech-activity of every single individual and we have not established a gulf between 'language' and 'speech'.

When Saussure speaks of the study of a dead Language as something different from, or independent of, 'la parole', he again exaggerates the difference. A man learning the very deadest language can only do so by a mental process which is nearly allied to the manner in which he has taken his native language into his mind. And not only when he writes it, but when he reads it (and understands what he reads), his linguistic activity is an outcome of 'la parole'. If that expression has any meaning, it must embrace not only the 'extrinsic' linguistic effort, the effort to utter words and sentences, that is, to talk or otherwise impart something, but also the 'intrinsic' linguistic effort, the effort to catch a linguistic communication from others and receive it into himself. But this side has not been sufficiently emphasized by the authors we have named.

When Saussure says that the individual is always master over 'la parole', while he can neither make nor change 'la langue', this is a monstrous exaggeration. The individual, as a matter of fact, *can* make something new which has influence on the language, on the language of the whole community. This is of course the way in which the countless new formations and transformations which actually show themselves in the language come about. They appear first with the individual, in his 'parole', but they become generally received and recognized when all, or at least many, people in the same linguistic community have adopted them, that is to say, use them in their own speech, in their 'parole'. This, as has been mentioned, Saussure himself saw to be true in the case of some of the formations concerned, but he does not set the matter in the right light.

Again one may indeed say with Saussure that the individual is king of his own speech, he is free to distort words at pleasure and to make for himself the strangest possible new words. But, observe! if he passes very narrow bounds, it is hardly speech any longer, because — and here I touch on a main point — the most individual speech is socially conditioned: an individual is never completely isolated from his surroundings, and in every utterance of 'la parole' there is a social element. It is only when baby lies in his cradle and amuses himself with babbling without attaching any meaning to the sounds he makes, or when a grown man takes a solitary walk in the wood or by the sea and gives vent to his cheerful humour either by trolling a loud stave or humming meaningless sounds, only there do we get an activity of 'la parole' which is not socially conditioned. Otherwise every individual conforms more or less exactly to an external norm. One person talks as others talk. Our only reason for talking is to make an impression on others, we must therefore take account of their prejudices. Every individual therefore has a norm for his 'parole' given him from without: it is given him in fact by his observation of the individual 'paroles' of others. We can say then in a sense that language ('la langue') is a sort of plural to speech ('la parole') — a plural in the sense that 'many horses' is a plural of 'one horse', it signifies the one horse $+$ horse no. 2 which is slightly different from it, $+$ horse no. 3, a little different again, and so on. All the different individual-tongues together are the national language. At any rate we get this sort of addition-sum so far as the vocabulary is concerned, in as much as the vocabulary of a language includes all the words which are used by all the members of the speech-community taken together. With regard to other sides we may rather say that the national language is a sort of average of individual-tongues, for example with regard to grammar, including 'pronunciation', i. e. what is common in the sound-forms of words. Here from many individual-tongues which differ slightly from one another we have extracted a common concept, just as we have the common concept 'horse', with which no single existing horse agrees in a single point, if we look carefully. Seeing then that Saussure's 'parole' and 'langue' are only two sides of the same thing, and that both are forms of human effort, and both — be it remarked — human effort socially coloured, we come to set up another and a more promising antithesis, 'individual-language' and 'collective-language' — language in the individual and language in the nation.

Still the subject is not exhausted: something remains in the background which is hinted at but not developed in Saussure's distinction. When 'la parole' is defined as the action of a single person, it is indeed only his linguistic functioning at a single moment. When he says 'horse', he has not in his mind or at any rate he has not in his 'speech', at the same moment, a bull or an appletree or football. In the definition of language ('langue') on the other hand Saussure speaks of the sum of the word-pictures that are stored in the mind of all individuals. But what about the word-pictures that are stored in the mind of a single speaker? Are they 'language' or 'speech'? do they belong to 'la parole' or to 'la langue'? This is not told us, and yet in the definition of the nature of language, the existence of these individual storehouses is assumed. This shows, as I think, a certain narrowness in the point of view. We can perfectly well 'represent' the stock of the single individual in a dictionary and a grammar. We have, as a matter of fact, Homeric dictionaries and Homeric grammars, and the same in the case of Shakespeare and other outstanding writers. From the present point of view, there is no great difficulty in it. If 'speech' in the most proper and strictest sense is the momentary linguistic functioning of the individual, in nearer or more distant agreement with the linguistic usage of the people around him, that is still not the end of the matter. Humboldt says somewhere that language is not merely *das sprechen* but also *das gesprochen haben;* we may add, *das gehört haben*. In every single person's mind there lie, thrust into the background at the moment, many memories of previous linguistic experiences: what is meant by saying they 'lie' there, is for the psychologists to explain: the rest of us take memory as a fact we cannot get away from. But these linguistic elements there in the background are at the same time potential linguistic agencies. They rest on something in the past, they are latent in the present, but they have a side which turns to the future. When the occasion presents itself, they can be transformed into linguistic agencies, into actual words and sentences. They are there and they are *not* there, just as an author's thoughts and a composer's airs are, and are not, in the book or the written notes: they are not actual

thoughts or actual sounds till the moment when someone reads the book, or plays the notes. Till then the
author's words and the composer's airs are arrested
and numbed on their passage from mind to mind;
they are like the frozen bugle-notes in Baron Münch-
hausen which had to be thawed before they could
be heard.

And so we reach a new duality, the distinction
between the actual and the potential. When a word
is pronounced, we have an actual linguistic action con-
sisting of many successive links: the thought that is
to be expressed, the apprehension of the sound or
group of sounds which must be produced to express
it, and finally the movements of the organs of speech
themselves. And when the word is heard by someone else, we have again an actual linguistic action,
but of another kind: the movement of the air produced by the first action are received by the ear,
transformed in the brain into a sound-perception, which
again is transformed into a thought or concept, into
something that corresponds more or less closely to that
which was the starting-point of the first person's action. But a word, as it lies unused in the brain or
as it stands in a dictionary s a *potential* linguistic action: which corresponds to, and can be transformed
into, actual linguistic activity of the kind just described.
Both words, however, the actual and the potential,
are socially conditioned. An uttered group of sounds
has no linguistic value, belongs not to language, is
therefore neither a word nor a sentence, unless it is
adapted to call up a memory-picture of earlier uttered
sound-groups, to which some meanings were attached.

If I say 'finatjuskskia' with which neither I myself, nor anyone else so far as I know, connects any thought, my action comes indeed under Saussure's concept 'parole', but it falls outside what I should call either speech or language, because the social element is lacking. If on the contrary I link a thought to this word, if for me it means 'bread-and-butter' or 'excellent' or 'go away' or anything you like, so that on another occasion I can use it in the same sense, and it becomes a habit with me, then indeed in my individual dialect it has become a word. It is then possible that people around me when they hear me use this strange collocation of sounds, will be able to gather from the situation what I mean by it, and so it may become a constituent part of the dialect of our family or of our nearer friends. If this happens it has now acquired the social stamp necessary before it can belong to a language. It can then, thanks to imitation, spread to wider and wider circles, to the whole town, the whole district, the whole nation, to the whole of humanity.

By way of repetition and imitation we have therefore got the single action converted into custom and habit. And so in the world of language there are the important stages: action, custom, habit. The language of a nation is the set of habits by which the members of the nation are accustomed to communicate with one another.

*

The investigation has been perhaps a little in the domain of abstract theory, though, I hope, not too difficult to follow. At any rate I considered it necessary in order to clear our ideas. In the course of it we have grasped the following points, which must never be let go if one would hope to understand what language is: individual momentary actions of a particular kind — agreement between these individual actions and actions previously performed by the same individual, individual customs — agreement between customs of one individual and customs of another This last agreement is brought about by what is called imitation, which accordingly is a fundamental condition if an action or custom which had belonged to a single person is to belong to a number of persons, is to be common to the members of a community great or small, in other words is to become social. So action —custom—imitation, on the one side: the individual— a smaller circle—a larger circle, on the other side. The alpha and omega of the life of a language is all *there*.

The influence of imitation in human society can hardly be overestimated. We speak of 'human apes and put into the words all the scorn we have for our nearest animal cousins. But what if the animal-psychologists are right who deny to apes the faculty of real imitation, in any case the faculty of learning anything by imitation, and maintain that imitation is a prerogative of Man! It is assuredly not always a bad thing that men imitate one another. Imitation is not merely picking up silly fashions and echoing idiotic phrases: a good example may be just as infectious as a bad one. Without imitation, there can be no civilized life, at any rate no linguistic life. If a child did not try to the best of its ability to talk like grown-up people or like children rather older than it, it would be permanently shut out from the common life of the spirit and really remain outside the human society. But even the grown man or woman imitates his neighbours' speech, consciously or unconsciously. Involuntarily one is disposed to make any motion that one sees made by someone else, it is well known that one may begin to yawn just because one sees some one else yawning, or merely sees some one else moving his thumb and finger up and down with an opening gesture. There is something called an instinctive fellow-feeling with others: often not visibly manifested, but at work in secret, in tiny innervations of the muscles. Pianists will tell you that they sometimes get tired in the arms with merely hearing other people play with too tense muscles of the arm and wrist. There is a good deal to be said for the theory, advanced in his day by Stricker and since much canvassed by psychologists, that the way in which most people understand the speech of others is by transmutation of perceptions of sound, something purely acoustic, into perceptions of articulations, the hearer softly to himself innervating slightly the same muscular movements that would be called into play if he was to say aloud what he heard. When we hear a song sung, we join in, though inaudibly. And what one has done in concert with another, one can do afterwards when alone, and very often one will do it again without knowing that it is not original. It is not easy to distinguish between what one has derived from others and what one has oneself originated. The words we read in *Faust*:

'You think you shove, and lo, they're shoving *you*

[1] 'Du glaubst zu schieben und du wirst geschoben.'

apply in their fullest extent to the life of language. But they apply to such an extent that we believe we are being shoved even when we ourselves are joining in the shoving, just as when we are in a disorderly crowd and without any will of our own are pressing others and being pressed ourselves. One is swept along with the speech-habits of the community — and at the same time without knowing it one may come to bring out something quite new, which others perhaps may take up and elaborate further. This is that mutual active and passive force for which Englishmen have the excellent expression 'give and take': We mutually give and take! And we do not always know where the one ends and the other begins.

CHAPTER II

INFLUENCE OF THE INDIVIDUAL

On the question of the influence of the individual on changes in language we have a very valuable treatise *L'unité phonétique dans le patois d'une commune*[1] by L. Gauchat. The author's object is to investigate individual differences in sound in a French-speaking Swiss commune near Bulle in the Canton Fribourg. In as much as the population is very much isolated and the influence of literary French is infinitesimally slight (at any rate so far as sound is concerned, syntax and vocabulary are more affected), one might have expected to find great uniformity in the pronunciation. Gauchat on the contrary discovered very great differences which in spite of the great area of the commune did not correspond to differences of locality (p. 226). On the other hand in the next commune, three miles distant, he was astonished to find exactly corresponding variants in sound, distributed just in the same way, though there is scarcely any intercourse between the two communes. The most important

[1] In the *Festschrift Morf.* 1905.

differences were between speakers of different ages: if one took two old people in the two communes, their pronunciation was more alike than the pronunciation of either was like the pronunciation of the young people in his own commune. In the case of the sound-shiftings which he studied with particular care, he found a marked difference between the quite old people, from 60 to 90, who only knew the old sound, the intermediates in age, from 30 to 60, who used both sounds, either indiscriminately, or one sound in certain words and combinations, another in others, and lastly the young people under 30 who used only the new sound. Women were often more inclined to use the new sound than men of approximately the same age, and Gauchat is disposed to ascribe to women a great influence on changes of sound, they having more to do with the next generation than men who go out to their work early and are tired and disinclined to talk when they come home.

What part then does the individual speaker play in these sound-shiftings? Do they start with the individual and spread from him to others in ever-widening circles? Gauchat decidedly thinks not: 'The individual counts for nothing in this phonetic development. The first individual who said *du pā* instead of *dow pā* did not make the others follow his example. It simply was not remarked'. (p. 202). His material shows him no trace of personal influence, and as he puts it roundly: 'J'ai étudié, d'une façon sommaire, environ 50 langues individuelles et je n'y ai rien trouvé d'individuel' (p. 231).

This is a great exaggeration. One can find even in Gauchat utterances which might have served to correct his view. He declares himself (p. 193) that in the matter of vocabulary and use of words, individual influence counts for much: parents and companions get children to prefer one expression over a rival expression, and there are words peculiar to a family which may easily lead to the formation of nicknames. But if this individual influence is recognized in some domains, why make an exception of the domain of sounds, and of that alone? Gauchat (p. 207) even contradicts his own words. 'Instinctive imitation,' he says, 'especially on the part of children, contributes enormously to the diffusion of a new fashion *(mode)* of articulation, so much the more as the new fashion of pronunciation is generally, (though not always) easier. Imagine to yourself a much frequented path which makes a great circuit: one fine day it occurs to someone or other to take a short cut across a meadow. The owner makes no objection. Very soon a number of people follow the new track, and at last the old circuitous way is overgrown with grass, while the short cut is recognized universally.' Yes, that is just what does happen: someone makes a beginning — we may not be able to say who it is — and others, more and more of them, follow him. When, in answer to an imaginary opponent who assumes influence to be exerted by an individual, Gauchat asks ironically, on what such a superiority should rest: 'Must one be the child of a rich man or of a schoolmaster in order to play a part in linguistic evolution?' the answer will be easy to anyone who has closely observed the behaviour of children when they are together or at play. He must have noticed that

there is always one or more who make themselves of
importance among their fellows, influence them, and
decide what the game shall be and how it shall be
played. But also this as a rule has nothing to do
with the social standing of the parents, but rests on
the character of the particular children. Some are by
nature more adapted than others to be masters and
leaders even in little things, and these are imitated,
consciously and unconsciously, by the others.

*

As against the influence of an individual, Gauchat
would maintain that a change like that of *ow˙* to *u*
was quite natural, ('était dans la nature des choses')
and must have happened many times ('elle a dû se
répéter indéfiniment' p. 202) and that 'the error of
saying *du pã* cannot become a law till it has been
made independently by a great many individuals'. In
all this however there is nothing that tells against individual initiative. We are merely told that a change
in sound has the best chance of winning the day if it
arises spontaneously in many people who have no
connexion with one another. The cause may be one
of many different things, easiness of production, the
whole construction of the language (its stock of sounds
and stock of words) which brings it about that shiftings can be more easily uttered at one point than at
another point, [1] etc., etc.: circumstances which we

[1] This is the sort of thing which is at the bottom of 'that
mysterious tie which unites the evolution of the two villages'
(Gauchat, p. 228). In order to understand the agreement in shiftings
of pronunciations within a larger or smaller linguistic community

are not always, or rather, which we are very seldom, lucky enough to be able to lay our finger upon. But exactly the same more or less hidden agency operates in other domains than that of sounds, and operates in exactly the same manner. In every case the individual to whom in the last resort the change is to be referred, only gets followers if he is in agreement with something which can also carry weight with others. The one individual, the other individual: it is only by their collusion that something of lasting importance can come into being: that is what we mean when we speak of language as 'un fait social'.

Why then is Gauchat so unwilling to admit individual influence in the domain of sounds while he admits it in other domains? The reason is perhaps — he does not expressly say so, but one dare at any rate opine it — that sound-changes occur without the individuals being conscious of them, whereas changes of other kinds, the springing up of a new word and the like, do not pass so unobserved. He declares (pp 202, 231) how astonished the inhabitants of his village were when he showed them that they did not all talk alike. They would get angry and protest: 'nous parlons tous la même chose'. Perhaps however it is not right to attach so much importance to this. The people whom Gauchat talked with on these variations of speech were probably all grown up, and it is a fact that grown-up peasants — for the matter of

one must not postulate mystical powers which so operate that all the children born at a given time in one and the same place come into the world without the capacity to articulate this or that sound, for example, *l mouillé*, and so substitute for it 'y'.

that, almost all grown-up people who have not been regularly trained to linguistic observation — have been blunted to such trifles as their own habits of speech and those of the people around them. Grown up people are interested in what is said, not in how it is said, (a fact which by the way applies to morphology and syntax as much as to sounds). But it does not follow that the same thing is true of children, who at the very age at which one does not speak to them of such things, are extraordinarily observant of points of language, and who certainly when very young make a mass of observations on language, which later recede into the background of their minds. Evidences of the reflexion and consciousness of children at the age at which they are learning their mother-tongue I have already given in my book on Child's Language and in *Language*, where observations of others beside myself are also adduced. So, with all thanks to Gauchat for what he has observed, we may be allowed to interpret the information he gives us in a way of our own, that is, to ascribe to the individual a greater influence even on the development of sounds than Gauchat will admit. [1]

---

[1] On the question of the influence of children on the development of language, Gauchat's attitude is against ascribing to them a preponderating influence (p. 228 ff). On p. 213 he says he believes 'que le langage fait un pas décisif en avant avec chaque changement de génération, mais la première impulsion, celle qui entraine tout le mouvement, doit résider dans le parler des adultes. L'enfance n'est d'abord qu'imitative, elle prend part à l'évolution en imitant mal, mais la langue commencera à se déformer et à se reformer définitivement quand les organes se seront affermis et que la nouvelle génération sera entrée en pleine et libre possession de sa langue.' Is not there some self-contradic-

Again, the individual may exert an influence, where it is not a matter of his having originated something, but of his having introduced something from elsewhere. Two examples are quoted by H. Schurtz.[1] In a little town in the Erzgebirge he had occasion to notice that a lady who had come from Leipzig had brought the pronunciation of *k* as *g* into the best society, so that it was considered *chic.* And Karl Braun, he tells us, has a similar story of a little town in Nassau where the women, following a lady who set the fashion, considered it the last thing in refinement to pronounce *i* as *ü*.

*

When therefore an innovation, be it a turn, a word or a syntactic peculiarity is adopted into a language, it is not the case that it springs up all at once in a mystical 'folk-mind', it always starts from an individual. It belongs to the individual before it becomes the possession of the 'folk'. One may compare the way in which popular ballads arose. Grimm thought they originated in a mystical or half-mystical way: they were made by the 'folk' itself in contrast to works of 'art-poetry' each of which was composed by a single man, generally pen in hand and alone in his chamber.

tion between the words that 'les organes seront affermis', and that that is the time when the transformation of the language begins? In *Language* p. 166 ff. I tried to show on purely linguistic grounds that some changes in languages can, or may, be ascribed to the carrying over of the language to a new generation in contrast to other changes which can, or may, have originated with speakers of the language *after* they had acquired their mother tongue.

[1] *Urgeschichte der Kultur,* 1900, p. 481.

However one must not consider the distinction as holding good absolutely. Even in a quite primitive community we know of something which can be compared with our protection of artistic copyright. I shall only adduce two pieces of evidence for this, but they come from places widely apart. In the Andaman Islands everyone composes his own tune and it is considered a breach of etiquette to sing anyone else's tune. [1] Similarly, William Thalbitzer in his magnificent new great book [2] says in speaking of the Drum-songs of Greenland, that a poem is called its author's *pia*, that is, his property. It would not be considered fair if anyone else should recite or sing a poem while the author was still alive.

The theory which explains the origin of popular ballads by 'das volk dichtet' ('the folk is the poet') has been espoused in our day by some American investigators, headed by F. B. Gummere. He speaks of 'communal origin of poetry' just as Wundt and others speak of a 'folk-mind' or 'collective spirit' — both believe in the complete homogeneity of the community which created the ballads. However in an able investigator like G. L. Kittredge, who appears to support that view, one will find a less mystical explanation. He imagines that ballads arose in a more natural manner. Thus, in a gathering of people met together for a dance, one begins to improvise. The line he has uttered is taken up and repeated and perhaps added to by another, and so on, till the refrain composed by the first of them is repeated in chorus by the whole company of dancers.

[1] Hagen, see Bücher, *Arbeit und Rhytmus* p. 54.
[2] *The Ammassalik Eskimo* (Copenhagen 1923), p.159.

The whole is remembered and used on later occasions, sometimes in exactly the same form, but more often with larger or smaller variations, due to imperfect recollection or to more or less conscious embellishment. And so by oral transmission it is carried far and wide. Even though every single phrase in the ballad is thus originally due to an individual, all traces of individual composition have now vanished, and to this extent one can say 'das volk dichtet'. And so much the more as the ballads contain a number of common features, whole lines or stock expressions which the improviser has always ready to hand, and which the whole party know and remember, and use when occasion offers, but which are no more the property of any single person than the common phrases which are in the mouths of all of us, such as 'that depends upon circumstances'.[1]

The creation of new words and turns of speech is not quite on a par with the folk-poetizing sketched above. But there are points of likeness in the two processes. The individual leader, having a greater gift for language than his fellows, comes out with something previously unknown. If it departs too widely from what others know and recognize, it dies a natural death, often perhaps because it is not at once understood, and the man has therefore to repeat his thought in a more intelligible form. If on the other hand the

---

[1] Gummere, *Old English Ballads*; *The Beginnings of Poetry;* chapter in the *Cambridge Hist. of Eng: Lit.*; Kittredge in Sargent and Kittredge, *Engl. and Scottish Popular Ballads*, Introd. Against the theory of communal origin many dissertations by Louisa Pound, most recently in *Publ. Mod. Lang. Assoc.* XXXIX, p 440. ff. (1924). Cp. also A. Olrik, *Nogle grundsætninger for sagnforskning* (1921) pp. 38, 155.

word or expression meets with a response, finds its sounding-board in the mind of the other, then it is remembered, and can be used again when the occasion arises. Every repetition helps it to establish itself — and so perhaps it spreads to wider and wider circles, till at last it is the spiritual possession of the whole community, nay, of the whole people.

But every time that the expression is repeated by a new person, he re-creates it, and so becomes a joint-creator, jointly responsible for it, the more so as very often at the moment he uses it, he does not clearly or precisely remember where or from whom he heard it before — he is merely conscious that there is such a word or such an expression. A new expression naturally has the best chance of making its way in this manner when it agrees so naturally with the whole constitution of the language, that it may easily be started by different people quite independently of one another.[1] This applies for example to a great extent in analogy-formations, new derivatives formed after a model, such as are found in language in multitudes.

We may say then theoretically that one man must naturally have been the first to employ the new expression, and is therefore in a certain sense its originator, but the other people who use it later use it, not because they have heard and learnt it from *him*, — they need never have known him — but because it comes so ready to hand and there is no question of the first man's 'artistic copyright'. Such a word or expression is from the very first that

[1] So also Delacroix L P p. 187.

which other words or expressions come to be in the end — the property of the whole people. It is the people which has not only sanctioned it, but created it And still we need not imagine to ourselves a mystical common folk-mind.

CHAPTER III

DIALECT AND COMMON LANGUAGE

Leaving the individual, we turn to the study of linguistic communities. These are of different magnitudes and may be arranged in an ascending series — the family, the clan, the tribe, the people or nation, and finally the super-nation, by which term we mean such a linguistic community as the English-speaking community with its 150 millions distributed over five continents. One cannot of course draw sharp dividing lines, for example between the tribe (the term is most used of uncivilized beings) and the people, but our inability to do so will not in this sphere prejudicially affect a scientific view of the case.

Family life has in many ways a strongly unifying effect within the narrower circle, but in return a highly separative effect in regard to those outside the circle. Every family has a certain tendency to acquire a language of its own with its own expressions, pet names and nick-names, and indeed with words and sentences of its own which are either not known at all or not known in that particular meaning outside the family-circle. This certainly has a bearing on the fact that closely related languages often diverge from one another noticeably in their expressions for such notions as 'boy' and 'girl' which there is so much occasion to talk about in family life. Thus 'dreng', 'pige' — 'gut', 'jente', — 'gosse', 'flicka', — 'horra' 'grøbba' — 'boy', 'girl', — 'knabe', 'mädchen', — and in the chief Romance languages — 'garçon', 'ragazzo', 'fanciullo', 'muchacho', 'mozo'.

The etymologies of many of these words are obscure: some show strange changes of meaning (*dreng* meant originally a long pole, *mozo* is said to be from the lat. *musteus*, belonging to must or new wine, and so fresh, young) and they therefore bear the stamp of having been originally jocose words or slang. Such words are just the ones which were likely to spring up and ramify in a family circle.

It must however be pointed out that no one belongs exclusively to his family. Every single member of the circle also comes in contact with many people outside it. This is especially the case when life is as varied and many-sided as it is today. Most people at present spend only a comparatively small part of their time in the bosom of the family. The separative influence of family-life is therefore counteracted in many different ways.

Those who have studied the way of life and the language of wild tribes have often pointed out to what an incredible degree these are often split up. This holds especially of the hotter countries (cp. *Language* p. 181 ff.). In their book on the Melanesian language

(p. 492) Gabelentz and Meyer show that almost every single village on the Maclay Coast (in the N. E. of New Guinea) has its own dialect, so that even villages a mile apart have many different words, while villages 6 or 8 miles apart can hardly understand one another. If you take a journey of a day or more, you need two, sometimes three, interpreters. Churchill declares similarly that Melanesia is 'a tangle of severally incomprehensible languages. In my study of that major division of Pacific I have made use of more than a hundred distinct tongues . . . Even so tiny an islet as Three Hills — it is but six miles long — has two distinct and severally incomprehensible languages'. (Beach-la Mar, p. 8). According to Curr there are more than 200 Australian dialects to some few thousand inhabitants. On the Timor Island it has been reckoned that there are 40 dialects to 100,000 individuals (Niceforo GA p. 214).

*

In the civilized countries best known to us we do not find the same degree of 'splitting' as among primitive tribes. Even here however we find in historical times great dialectal differences within what may be considered the 'same language', inhabitants of different districts in the same linguistic area having difficulty at times in making themselves mutually understood. Recent investigations have shown that in many places it is difficult to indicate sharp boundary lines. That is to say, if we take a line as a frontier between two dialects, we do not find a multitude of linguistic phenomena (of sounds, of grammar, of vocabulary) which once and for all mark off district A from the neighbouring district B. As a rule we find that the frontiers for one phenomenon do not exactly coincide with the frontiers for another, so that the 'isoglosses' (as such frontiers of single phenomena are called) sometimes agree, sometimes run somewhat parallel with one another, but fairly often cross one another in the most distracting manner. The dialect-atlases which of recent years have appeared in many countries have especially opened our eyes to this state of things and have led to a lively discussion of the causes of the many-coloured pictures which philologists have thus presented to us. But for the purpose before us, it is not necessary to go into the matter more closely. We may be content to say that in spite of the gradual transitions found in many districts, especially in flat districts in which the population is evenly distributed, there still are such things as dialects in the geographical sense.

When I speak of dialects as determined by facts of geography, this must not be taken in a too physical sense. The most important cause of a language splitting into dialects is not purely physical, but want of communication for whatever reason. The great highroads, including the old Roman roads and broad military roads, have counteracted dialect-splitting. It has been pointed out that navigable rivers are not natural hindrances conditioning dialectal differences — (see below, of the Sound) while a broad river like the Garonne did in old days separate the people on its two banks and led to marked differences of language. Again in mountainous districts linguistic frontiers are not always determined by the highest peaks or watersheds. Very often the passes allowed of such a brisk intercourse between the populations on the two sides of the high mountains, that linguistic unity was completely or at least tolerably preserved. On the other hand forests were in many places a cause of linguistic differentiation: in primitive times they were quite impassable. According to P. K. Thorsen[1] the strongly marked division between the dialects of East and West Jutland is due to the fact that in ancient times there was an uninhabited tract of forest between the two, a belt in which no antiquarian remains have been found, whereas many have been found in the districts east and west of the line. Similarly Gunnar Knudsen[2] has shown that in South Seeland a dialect frontier follows the line of an old forest-tract, which is also comparatively destitute of early remains.

Where, as in most of north-west France, there were not natural hindrances of this sort to make intercourse in early days impossible, we see one dialect gradually and evenly shading into another, and so-called 'isoglosses' crossing one another, without any sharp division anywhere between dialects which are markedly different in many respects. On the contrary the sharp division of Danish and German in Slesvig and Holstein is explained perfectly naturally by the fact of a broad forest-track having been there in old days: the name Holstein contains as its first element *holt* (wood).

It is therefore *human* geography which is the decisive factor in the formation of dialects. In France it has been pointed out that ecclesiastical divisions had a great effect on language. In the old dioceses religious observances

[1] *Gjedved seminarium* 1862—92 p. 105 ff.
[2] *Sydsjællandske stednavne* p. 29.

caused men to congregate about one centre and so cut them off from other districts. I will not go into the matter more closely. I only wished to show very briefly in what sense dialects can be called geographical units.

*

In the life of language we seem to see two opposing tendencies, the one in the direction of splitting, the other in the direction of larger and larger units. Which tendency is the stronger? Most of the writers on the science of language we read leave us with the impression that the natural process of evolution is steadily in the direction of splitting and cleavage, so that out of unity arises variety. I need only refer to one living philologist who says this in express terms, I mean H. C. Wyld. He strongly disputes the belief that the tendency of language is in the direction of unity, and maintains that it is in the direction of 'infinite variety'. In this he is only one of many, and those of us who cling to the possibility of an artificial international language are ever having it dinned in our ears that such a language will be of no use, because in a short time it will split into a number of languages in the same way that natural languages have done. The argument is extremely weak. In the first place an artificial language which is almost exclusively used for international intercourse is not governed by the same laws of life as natural languages; and secondly one may just as well say that it is of no use to talk or write English (for example) because according to the theory this language will also soon break up. People have been struck by the fact that in many areas we see

a number of languages springing from what was one
language before; the Scandinavian language which was
once common to all has split into Icelandic, Færoic,
Norwegian, Swedish and Danish. In historical times
Portuguese, Castilian, Catalonian, Provençal, French,
Italian, Roumanian have sprung from Latin, and something of the same sort may be seen in the Slavonic and
Keltic languages. If we go further back we see the
common Aryan or Indo-European language break up
into a number of different languages. It has been the
same with common Semitic, with common Ugro-Finnic
etc. Are we not face to face with a universal law of
nature which is valid at all times and over the whole
globe? Well, so think most linguists, as has been said.
With what one might call a fatalistic belief, they put
forward this side of the question without seeing that
there are also forces working in exactly the opposite
direction, and completely overlooking the fact that these
unifying forces have in historical times been really
stronger than the differentiating forces, that they are
so particularly at present, and certainly will be so in
the future.

Here I would call attention to the fact that the ordinary doctrine of the strength of the cleavage-tendency
rests to some extent on an optical illusion, which is
connected with our habit of counting *languages* and
thinking of them as existing independently of the
people who speak them. There can be no doubt that
the world has never been more thickly inhabited than
it is at present. In early times when we had the
common Scandinavian language, the common Romance
(Latin), the common Slavonic, which we have spoken

of, and so on, there was only a very meagre population to speak any of these languages. If we reckon
it out thus: whereas at that time a single million of
people perhaps — (the number is mere guesswork, I
admit) — were scattered over the Scandinavian countries and talked a common Scandinavian speech, there
are now about three millions talking Norwegian, six
millions Swedish, and three millions Danish — do we
not see that there is really a larger linguistic community
than there was 1000 years ago? The contrast is still
more striking if we compare the insignificant number
of people who before the beginning of our era talked
what was the according to the general view the common
West-Gothonic or West-Germanic language, with the
150 millions who now talk English, the 75 millions who
now talk German and the 10 millions who now talk
Dutch or Flemish. Spanish alone (in Spain and in
America) is spoken by a far larger number of people
than Latin was when the Roman Empire ruled the
world, and the same is the case both with French and
Italian. There is indeed — at any rate over great parts
of the globe — an enormous tendency towards one and
the same language being spoken by a far larger population than at any earlier time in the world's history.

*

The greatest and most important phenomenon of
the evolution of language in historic times has been the
springing up of the great national common-languages —
Greek, French, English, German etc. — the 'standard'
languages which have driven out, or are on the way
to drive out, the local dialects purely conditioned by

geographical factors. The tendencies to 'splitting' having been counteracted, linguistic forms are created so far independent of place, that the person using them does not betray by his speech where he comes from.[1]

The factors that have governed the great national evolution of language in earlier and more recent times, and the relation of a standard language to local dialects, have occupied the attention of many learned investigators. As a rule however these have concerned themselves only with a single language. An attempt will now be made to get a synthetic and comprehensive view of the most important factors which — though in rather different ways and especially with different degrees of strength in different countries — have operated everywhere where a standard language has arisen.

Linguistic unity depends always on intercourse, on a community of life, whereby the chief roughnesses of different dialects are smoothed down. What disappears is for the most part those peculiarities which people first notice in others and are inclined to make fun of. But this intercourse may be assisted or brought about in various ways. The intercourse which has a decisive effect may be due in some cases to a *war* causing the mingling of populations from different parts of the country. Again it may be due to something of a more peaceful nature. It is said that the establishment of an annual fair in the Rocky Mountains has had the result that the Indian tribes to east and west which at first

[1] I proposed in 1890 as a definition of the best Danish the speech of those by whose pronunciation one cannot hear what part of Denmark they come from. (*Dania* I. p. 41, repeated in *Fonetik* 1897 p. 93, and in *Phonetische Grundfragen* where it is fully argued out.)

could not understand one another, have now got nearer to one another in speech. [1]

Some investigators have laid great stress on the importance of marriages in the evolution of language, and have even given statistics to show the difference between villages where there was little marrying with people outside, and where consequently the old village-speech could persist unchanged and untouched, and other places whose inhabitants were more inclined to marry women from outside and where consequently speech changed with greater rapidity, local peculiarities having been more largely abandoned in favour of the standard language. See especially A. L. Terracher, *Les aires morphologiques. Étude de géographie linguistique*. Paris 1914; and cp. Meillet in *B S L* XIX p. 28 ff.

The eminent Dutch psychologist of language, van Ginneken, who discusses Terracher's book with great thoroughness in an article 'De schoondochters in de taalgeschiedenis' (*De nieuwe Taalgids* 10) was himself strong on the same point before Terracher. In his *Handboek d. ned. taal* p. 337 he says: 'There is no better way of diffusing a cultivated common-language, (het Algemeen-Beschaafd), than by marriages between couples who talk different dialects. As a rule in such cases both parents, as a matter of course, talk the standard-language habitually at home. At any rate the children learn it. For it is noticeable how in these cases father and mother make it a point of honour to teach their children standard Dutch, and how ashamed they are if their toddling children repeat a dialect-word which slipped from their tongue at some careless moment.'

[1] Gallatin, quoted by Sayce, *Princ. of Comp. Philol.* p. 86.

Van Ginneken is filled with scorn for the philologists who have written reams on the whole subject of mixed languages without ever taking account of the fact th at the people married, and that it might well have some influence on the evolution of language *whom* they chose for husbands or wives. 'What man of science,' he asks ironically, 'would waste his time on such foolery? Fancy, such was the state of the question before A. D. 1914' ('Kom, welk wetenschappelijk man verbeuzelde z'n tijd nu aan zulke futeliteiten! . . . Heusch, zoo was de stand der kwestie vóór het jaar onzes Heeren 1914').

We may be permitted to doubt if Terracher's point of view has contributed to science anything so decisively new and epoch-making in its truth as van Ginneken thinks.

In the first place, the fact which has been noticed, i. e. the unequal power of the standard-language to make itself felt in different districts cannot be exclusively due to a greater or less disposition to outside marriages. We must go deeper to find the real cause and must maintain that these external marriages and the linguistic changes are alike due to the same social and psychological facts. A population which for one reason or another has more to do with the world around and avoids getting isolated will be more disposed both to marry people outside and to talk with people outside, and so be brought to drop the specially local peculiarities which were found in village-speech at an earlier date. Terracher himself observes that the oldest dialect-frontiers which can be shown to exist in the region which he has specially investigated (Angoulème) do not coincide with the boundaries of parishes, or even of departments or provinces or other

administrative or juridical districts, but with those of
the old medieval feudal manors. They were therefore
determined by the old system of villenage according to
which the peasants were serfs tied to their lord's land
and not permitted to remove elsewhere or marry with
women of other manors. It was only with the abolition
of the old feudal restrictions on the right of the individual to determine his own career that the standard
language could make real headway among peasants.

And secondly, the theory put forward by Terracher
and van Ginneken attaches too much weight to the influence of the parents (or of the mother) on the form of
language used by the children. In my books *Børnesprog* and *Language* (p. 146 ff.) I have pointed out that
the language used by the child is determined far more
by that of its playfellows than by that of its parents.
I have seen many examples of this in families in Denmark in which the mother's Norwegian or Swedish
speech has had no appreciable influence on the children,
who have picked up their Danish from the people
around them. Let me now add to what I have said
before a mention of a case adduced by Anker Jensen. [1]
In a family of five members in the town of Åby in
East Jutland the father talks Standard Danish, the mother
West Jutlandish, the eldest daughter used to talk the
Åby dialect till she came home six months ago from
the High-School where she learnt a mixed language,

---

[1] *Dania* V. 1898 p. 226. The whole article 'Sproglige forhold
i Aby sogn, Århus amt' ['The linguistic situation in the parish of
Åby, in the administrative district of Arhus'] is an early example
of an investigation into the linguistic situation of a whole country-
town of the kind that Gauchat and Terracher have made famous.

while the two youngest children talk Aby dialect of the purest water. [1]

*

In many places religion has played an important part, the great religious festivals and assemblies drawing people together from far and wide. Certainly in Greece the oracles of Delphi and Olympia which were visited by all Hellenes must have had a great effect even from the point of view of language. Along with these stand the Olympic Games, which were not only athletic gatherings but also had a religious significance. Elsewhere the Church also operates as a unifying power in regard to language, though on this point we must remark that when the Church employs some special sacred language which is not understood by the common people, this operates as far as it goes in the contrary direction. The Catholic Church both in the past and at present has had its one language, Latin, but just because this has been only the language of the church, that is, of the clergy, and not the language of the faithful or of the multitude, the use of one language did not prevent Latin from breaking up into the Romance languages.

*

[1] Something similar is related of two German children whom H. V. Clausen met at the German Paper-Factory of Kristiansdal, west of Haderslev, in South Jutland. In spite of their having come only recently from the heart of Germany they talked excellent South-Jutlandish. When they were asked where they had learnt it, they answered 'At school'. But considering that the language used in the school was then German, they must have meant 'from their South-Jutlandish schoolfellows'.

Another investigation of the same kind is P. Skautrup's 'Om folke- og sprogblanding i et vestjysk sogn' ['On the blending of population and language in a West-Jutland parish'] *Danske Studier*, 1921, p. 97 ff.

Literature plays no small part in the rise of a great common-language. I am not thinking so much of particular great writers as of literary intercourse in general. In earlier times it was the general belief that each of the great national languages had been formed by some particular great writer, Italian for example, by Dante, English by Chaucer, German by Luther and Danish by Christiern Pedersen. Later research has shown that these men did not exert the influence attributed to them. Each of them used in the main a language which in its essential features was already formed when he took it over. Unifying forces had been at work before these men had begun to write, and though they had never written a line, Italian and English and the other languages would have probably looked much the same in all essentials as they do now. Their chief importance lay in this that they gave a certain impetus to what was already moving. They were regarded as literary models, and the imitation of their literary excellences led to imitations of their language on the part of some who otherwise would neither have spoken nor written the common-language: their idiom came then to be known in wider circles than that of other private individuals. But when I speak of the influence of literature, I am thinking of something else, a literary society which may arise before the birth of a written literature. For indeed there may be such a thing as an *oral* literature which lives on on the lips of the people and is transmitted by virtue of an excellent memory. In a natural state men have such a memory, while we so-called civilized people rely far too much on printed and written notes. The natives of N. W. Queensland

are said to be able to remember a series of songs,
so long that it takes five nights to get through them
all, and what is more remarkable, in a language which
the reciter hardly understands. That the words are
remembered exactly has been established by W E.
Roth who compared the notes he had made in many
different tribes more than a hundred miles apart.

So von den Steinen assures us from Brazil that
every tribe there knows the songs of the neighbour-
tribes, though it does not understand them. It has
also been shown that in North America religious songs
are very faithfully transmitted from generation to generation without being understood.[1] Their memory
for poems that they understand is of course also better than ours, as has been remarked by Radlov with
regard to the poetical productions of Turkish tribes.

We know that in many countries singers and reciters used to travel from one tribe to another, from the
court of one petty king or prince to that of another, and
were everywhere well received and richly rewarded
for entertaining their hosts by the recitation of long
poems or stories. They were in many cases compelled
to compose or recite their poems in some kind of
common-speech which was equally well (or approximately so) understood everywhere. If there was something here or there which was not fully understood
at the moment, it did not spoil the pleasure of the
hearers — it might indeed help to cast an additional
half-mystical glamour over the poem. But in order
that the main part of the recitation should be understood, the reciters were obliged to drop the most un-

[1] Lévy-Bruhl F M 118.

intelligible elements of their own local dialect: while on the other hand, as they could not acquire the particular dialect of every district they went to, they accommodated themselves to the way of talking of a number of districts. In this way a poetical or literary language was formed, which was able to keep very faithfully to its original type.

In the Middle Ages there was a common-language of this sort in Ireland, evolved in great part under the influence of the professional *saga*-men or story-tellers ('fili'). Moreover, it may be remarked, this common-language was not only written, but spoken. [1] I imagine that in ancient times things were the same in England. *Scopas* travelled round to the courts of the petty kings, and the larger mansions, and there gave their songs, — songs which from the beginning were composed in a common poetical language, everywhere understood. This literary language is now generally called by scholars West-Saxon, but in a strict sense it is not West-Saxon. We are told over and over again in all the manuals that these poems were composed originally in Northern English (Northumbrian) and were afterwards all translated from this dialect into West-Saxon. It is highly improbable that this should be right. When King Alfred wrote and got his assistants to write his translations from Latin, and when the authors of the West-Saxon Chronicle wrote down their annals, they were writing a literary language which in many respects differed from the specially West-Saxon spoken language, which we know from other records and which in our textbooks is now called West-Saxon *patois*. What

[1] Thurnaysen, *Die Kelten* p. 15.

is called pure or strict West-Saxon is therefore not pure West-Saxon, but purified West-Saxon. It is in reality a Standard Language, soaring above all the local dialects of Old-English.

I believe then that the state of things in regard to literature and language in England and Ireland in the early Middle Ages was analogous with that which prevailed, as we know, in ancient Greece.[1]

All types of Greek literature, except tragedy, were created in the colonies between the 7th and the 5th century before Christ. But between these colonies there was an active intercourse.

The language found in these works of literature is never quite the same as that of a particular town: the old literary language has a dialectal stamp, but it has nothing that is in the proper sense local. These literary works were addressed not to a single town, but to a group of towns, and indeed to the whole of Greece. Every branch of literature evolved its special language, coloured by that of the district in which it first sprang up But in the 6th and 5th centuries educated Greeks understood literary texts though written in dialects widely apart: Greek literary language has its 'style' like all Greek Art it is no mere exact copy of the reality. The Homeric language, an Ionian stratum laid over an Æolian, is extremely artificial This is not surprising in poetry addressed to an aristocracy not bound to the glebe of any one town, and poetry produced by a class of singers who delivered

[1] Whatever I say of Greek is based almost exclusively on the masterly and thorough treatment of this question in A. Meillet, *Aperçu d'une histoire de la langue grecque*, Paris, 1913.

it and conserved it, but were also not bound to any particular district. The language of the lyrical Chorus is also extremely composite and artificial, simple words being avoided or artificially changed in form as $k\bar{e}r$ (the heart) into *kear*, which was hardly ever used in colloquial speech.

*

A literary influence of a very special kind is seen in modern times in the important position taken by touring companies of actors. When actors are bound to appear one week in one town and the next week in another, they cannot adopt the local pronunciation and language of each town in turn, and must therefore like the wandering minstrels of old evolve a language which will be intelligible everywhere. On the other hand their pronunciation is then considered a model and is widely imitated. It is also clear that a man who is listened to by hundreds of people in a single evening can exercise a greater influence than one who is only heard in the narrow circle of the family or by a few of his professional colleagues.

There can be no doubt that the facts that British theatrical companies nowadays tour with their pieces not only all round Great Britain but in North America and Australia, and that many American actors and actresses have made successful appearances in London, must have contributed, and must now be contributing, to preserve the linguistic unity of the different parts of the English-speaking world. Still greater assuredly has been the influence of touring companies in Germany, where the political divisions before 1870 allowed every part of the country to keep its provincial idioms, but where a sort of pattern-pronunciation is being evolved on the stage which has often been proposed for imitation. In many passages of Goethe's conversations with Eckermann one may see the importance attached in literary circles to the fact that this or that pronunciation was unsuitable for the stage The same point of view is found in Palleske, for example, and quite recently, more scientifically expressed,, in Siebs's book on German pronunciation. 'Theatre-German' ('Bühnendeutsch') is widely identified with 'the best German'.

*

Meanwhile movements towards literary unity can scarcely ever be dissociated from other movements in the same direction in the sphere of politics, settlement of the population etc. Most if not all of the standard languages whose origin is known to us owe their rise to a number of favourable conditions, in part very different in character, so that it is not possible to say precisely what influence has operated most strongly in each case. Social life depends on the joint-play of many different forces. This is very clearly to be seen in Ancient Greece.

Greece in the earliest period was divided into a number of little states, each with its local-speech, but already in the 4th century before Christ we see in inscriptions the influence of a common Ionian-Attic language. The Greeks did not, as the Indians did, set up a common learned language which got further and further away from the language of everyday life. Their literary languages always kept up a bond with the spoken language without being a mere reflexion of it. Even though the local dialects were often so different in character that it must have been difficult for people to understand one another in all details, the Greeks never entirely lost the feeling that they all spoke the same language. Herodotus is undoubtedly right in saying that five different Ionian languages were spoken in Asia Minor, but all the same the inscriptions found in the towns he names show practically no differences. Even at that time there was a sort of common-language, which as found in inscriptions was somewhat different from that used in literature of the same district, — a sort of official governmental language.

When in historical times we find that neighbouring districts differ very much in language, the reason lies in the fact that different races have been juxtaposed, in consequence of migrations and conquests. But along with the cleavage we find things that work in the direction of linguistic unity — I have already referred to popular gatherings for religious purposes and to literary languages. It made for unity that the Greeks in conquered or colonized districts had their settlements along the coast and did not push far up-country. The Hellenes' common Fatherland, as Meillet says, was the Sea, the whole of the Eastern Mediterranean, from Sicily to the Bosporus.

In later times, as is well known, a common Greek language, the so-called *koinē*, sprang up, partly as a written, partly as a spoken language. The *koinē*, from which the modern dialects have branched off, had rather a negative than a positive character: older features had been lost, and new ones had taken their place.

The sense of community came when the towns lost their political independence. Political power was in the hands either of kings, whose culture was Hellenic, but whose capitals lay outside Greece proper, or of a political union of many confederated towns. The cultivated classes everywhere now talked the same language, and local dialects if persisting at all were despised as plebeian.

As to what was the basis of this Late-Greek *koinē*, opinions are divided. Kretschmer[1] maintains that the Greek dialects in the course of their development from the earliest times converged towards one another, so that the earliest periods showed greater differences than the later. He sees in *koinē* a blending of the most different dialects, while Thumb[2] insists that it agrees with Attic, some Ionic features being thrown in, but very few from the other dialects. The difference between the two authorities is after all only one of degree — since neither maintains that *koinē* is a direct offspring of pure Attic.[3]

*

Sitzungsber. d. Wiener Akad. 1900, and somewhat less vehemently in Gercke and Norden's *Einleit. in d. altertumsw.* I, 523.

[2] In Streitberg's *Gesch.* 2. 116.

[3] Meillet expresses himself much in the same way as Thumb: 'La constitution de la *koinē* a comporté une atticisation de l'ionien, et c'est au modèle attique qu'on a visé à se conformer quand la *koine* s'est établie. Ce n'est pas dire que tout les menues particularités de l'attique aient été reproduites . . La *koinē* n'est pas de l'attiquè c'est du grec local plus ou moins atticisé . . . . L'influence d'Athènes n'a du reste été forte que durant les débuts de la constitution de la *koinē* . . . . . A l'epoque impériale, ce n'est plus Athènes qui fournit un modèle linguistique à qui veut parler grec: c'est Athènes qui accepte les formes communes'. (p. 336 f.)

The importance of the political situation in connexion with the question before us is extraordinarily great, as was indicated when we touched on the late Greek unity under the Macedonian kings. It is self-evident that where we have previously divided states combining under a single government, the chances of a common-language being evolved are so much the better. The court, the government have occasion for a language which will carry its message to all the inhabitants of the country, while on the other hand the seat of government naturally attracts people to it from all districts. The greatest uniformity in language is to be found where there is a markedly centralized government, as is evident in the old Roman Empire with its official Latin, and later similarly in France and to a great extent in England.

It is less easy for a common language to make its way in a country like Germany which for centuries was politically sub-divided and which had no capital. In consequence even now the colloquial language of educated Germans is more coloured by dialect than that of the educated people of most other European countries. Still Germany has not been utterly unaffected by tendencies working towards linguistic unity. Even before Luther's time there was the Saxon 'Chancery-language', which was imitated by other Chanceries, including those of Austria, and which became a sort of common official written-language. Later came Luther's translation of the Bible which, with its fresh natural style and with its choice of expressions which were not the sole property of a particular district, had great influence even in Catholic countries. The striving towards unity affected not merely the written, but also the spoken language. Here various influences made themselves felt: among others, that which has been put forward so strongly by E. A. Gutjahr[1] that spoken German was disseminated in the eastern regions where Slavonic had been previously spoken. German here was practically introduced by an upper class, and was talked rather formally, everyone having a feeling all through that he must talk correctly, and not 'let himself go' as he would in a little town in Saxony or Thuringia or Bavaria.

We come across something similar in other countries in which the language is used in its greatest purity in districts which were originally outside its range. Irishmen, we are told,[2] speak on the average better English ('nearer to the literary standard') than people of a corresponding class in England itself. In Cornwall and in the Scilly Islands, where Keltic was spoken till 150 years ago, I was struck by the 'pure' English talked by the peasantry, as compared for example with the dialect of the neigbouring county of Somerset. Gibbon in his *Memoirs* (p. 85) speaks of the purity of the French spoken in the Pays de Vaud.

[1] *Die Anfänge der neuhochdeutschen Schriftsprache*, Halle, 1910.

[2] Joyce, *English as we speak it in Ireland*, London 1910 p. 8.

CHAPTER IV

DIALECT AND COMMON LANGUAGE
(concluded)

The formation of a Common-Language is assisted by intercourse of any kind, so especially by military service. I may mention a characteristic incident recounted by the purist Dahl in his *Dansk hjælpeordbog*. He relates (p. 497) how in conversation with a peasant he had praised a number of old words which still lived on the lips of the people, but when he mentioned the word *tykkes*, the peasant answered, 'Yes, I know the word, but since I served as a soldier, I always say *synes*'.

In Germany the system of conscription has similarly assisted the evolution of a Common Language. Germans also maintain that the diffusion of the Common Language has been appreciably helped by the Prussian Government's having made it a rule to move its employés about as much as possible, so that after having been some years in the east, they should then spend some years in some districts of the west. Their own language — still more their children's language —

became more polished through the discarding of its local peculiarities.[1]

The Common Language is often in a marked degree a class-language, an upper-class language. This follows naturally from social conditions. The upper class travels more and mixes more with people of similar standing from other parts of the country. Consider the case of well-to-do English country-gentlemen, who even centuries ago went regularly once a year to London for 'the season' and 'high society', and who when they were at home on their estates were constantly receiving visits from friends and relations from other parts of the country. In either place social intercourse contributed to the disappearence of dialect. Add to this the effect of their boys being educated, not in day schools, but in the great 'public-schools' — boarding-schools for well-to-do boys from all parts. Accordingly Wyld and others have described Standard English now as 'class-dialect, independent of locality' and now as the natural speech of people who send their sons to 'public schools', that is, as 'the public school dialect'.

The same effect is produced, — and of course not in England alone but in most countries — by Universities, which seldom or never draw their students exclusively from one district. In some countries indeed, particularly Germany, it is even the custom for students not to be content to go to a single University, but to study at several in turn. We owe to Zarncke an interesting illustration of the manner in which the

[1] Palleske, *Kunst des Vortrags*, 2nd ed., 1884 p. 78 f. Palleske calls the language thus produced 'beamtendeutsch', ('civil service German').

higher educational institutions there bring people from different parts of the country into intimate relations with one another. Talking of Swiss students known to him who were studying at Leipzig and constantly associating with each other, he says that every one of them at first spoke the dialect of his particular canton, but in about six month's time a tolerably uniform language had been evolved. [1]

In Denmark not only the University and the other institutions for higher education at Copenhagen, but also the People's High Schools founded by Bishop Grundtvig have had great influence during the last fifty years in the same direction, — and, be it remarked, have had influence on a stratum of society otherwise most inclined to hold fast to local dialects, namely the peasants. 'It is astounding how quickly people learn to alter their language there. The effect is not merely due to the fact that the instruction is given in Standard Danish, but also — perhaps just as much — because the pupils of a High School come as a rule from different parts of the country so that each gets his or her speech polished by merely mixing with fellow-students'. [2] The High Schools produce their greatest effect on women.

In this connexion, as something that has also made for the evolution and diffusion of a Common Language, one may perhaps mention intelligence and education in general. Those who are mentally most alive will be disposed to take a wide outlook even in regard to language, so that they copy other people's ways and

[1] Quoted by R. Loewe, *Zeitschr. für Völkerpsychol.* XX p. 263.
[2] Anker Jensen, *Dania* V. p. 222.

come in touch with more people than those who have a narrower horizon.[1] This is confirmed by what we are told of peasant dialects or patois in Switzerland: they are to a greater degree on the way to be driven out by the standard language in the Protestant Cantons than in the Catholic, because in the former the school-system is better and the general level of intelligence is higher. (Dauzat, *Vie du langage* p. 206).

I have not yet mentioned one of the most important factors in the unification of language, viz. the rise of great towns. There can be no doubt that great towns like Athens and Rome played a notable

---

[1] Conversely, a man's way of talking is taken very widely as stamping his education or want of education and affects his whole position in society. This is especially the case in England where writers like Thackeray assert again and again the impossibility of a man of the higher classes marrying a girl who 'misplaces her h's'. In Gissing's *New Grub Street* a writer, Yule, marries beneath him, but is constantly put out by his wife's way of talking, and is driven wild if she merely says 'I've forgot' instead of 'I've forgotten'.

One may remark by the way that it is generally very small points that are fixed upon as objectionable, often insignificant things that hardly affect the value of the language as a means of communication: 'forgot' is just as intelligible as 'forgotten'. Further the standard changes — often in an unaccountable way — in course of time. In the 18th century 'forgot' and 'gotten' were recognized as good English, now in England it is considered right to say 'I have got', 'I have forgotten', while in America it is generally thought more correct to say 'I have gotten'. Some therefore of the points to which ordinary people attach importance may be really ascribed to narrowness of view, but all the same they play a great part in the general social judgment of language.

part in linguistic evolution, and would have done so quite apart from the political considerations already mentioned. But it has been the same thing all over the world in modern times. And this is quite natural. The growth of great towns is not due to the fact that the original population of towns was more fertile than that of country districts — it is rather the other way round. It rests on the fact that towns suck in a mass of people not only from their immediate environs, but from more remote districts. This can be shown by statistics. In my *Fonetik* (p. 96) I showed from the census-returns of 1890 that only 51 p. c. of the inhabitants of Copenhagen had been born in or near Copenhagen, while the corresponding percentage for Hillerød, a little town in Seeland, was 67, for the West-Jutland town, Ribe, 80, for a country district in Seeland, 89, and for an administrative division of West Jutland, 90. It naturally follows that in great towns the immigrants from different parts of the country get their dialect rubbed down in intercourse with one another, with the result that the population of a great town comes to talk in a manner which one would not expect from its geographical situation. And so we get the linguistic paradox that the common-speech of Athens was not pure Attic, the common-speech of Copenhagen is not pure Copenhagen, that of London not pure London, the French evolved in Paris not in the strict sense Parisian etc. The Common-Languages have been in the main evolved in Athens, Paris, London etc., but not by born Athenians, Parisians or Londoners.

*

So far as Copenhagen is concerned P. K. Thorsen has shown that the language there spoken in a number of points differs greatly from the Seeland dialect spoken around it, but agrees remarkably with the dialects of Bornholm and Skaane. We see also that the language spoken in the Danish fishing villages along the Sound is much more like the dialect of the fishing villages of Skaane across the water than that of the agricultural villages a mile or two inland.

Still more significant is what happened in England as shown in a number of recent investigations. Morsbach pointed out as early as 1888 that documents drawn up in London about the year 1380 and the years following show essentially the same forms as English written-language of a later date. The same linguistic form quickly spreads over the whole Kingdom, so that after the 15th century there are hardly any documents written in dialect. This common written-language, in most of its features though not in all, agrees with the language of the London-born poet Chaucer. Is it therefore to be called London-language?

One may answer yes, and no.

It is indeed possible that the writers of these documents employed already a half developed Common-Language just as the later scribes of the 15th and the 16th centuries often wrote standard English both at Lincoln and at Winchester. Dölle (1913) examined the oldest documents composed in London, but with meagre results. Heuser (1914) got more out of his investigation. He takes documents composed in London in French and Latin, especially wills, and notices the names of places and of persons occurring in them. He is thus able to point to various idiosyncracies of the old London dialect, e. g. O. E. *æ* here becomes *a*, not *e* as in English generally. The form -*strate* (street) is common. The features he has found agree most with place-names in Essex as given in the Doomsday Book, though some agree with place-names in Kent. Accordingly the original speech of London was East Saxon.

By his discovery of these characteristics Heuser is further enabled to establish the London origin of some texts which previously could not be assigned to any particular district. The most important is *Vices and Virtues*.

And now comes the interesting fact that in these London documents one can trace from decad to decad a constant breaking away from the local dialect, the forms previously most characteristic of London being driven out by forms previously only found in other districts, especially those of the North. The local dialect was able to hold its own in some names such as *Stepney*, *Lambeth*, *Kennington*, which were etymologically isolated, and so not understood. But the old London *Isemongerlane* was displaced by *Ironmongerlane*: *Crepelgate* persisted till the middle of the 16th century, but was then supplanted by *Cripplegate*. *Thames* keeps in writing the *a* of the London dialect, but this is pronounced *[e]*.

In other words, the language of the capital became less and less determined by locality, became more and more the English of England. This was natural with the enormous growth of the city, which came to be a real capital of the whole country, a centre for Court and trade, the meeting place of Parliament (Westminster was only just outside old London). From all districts noblemen and traders gathered here, attracted in ever greater numbers by the gaiety of the life and the prospects of gain.

It was, then, in London above all places that Standard English was evolved. But Standard English was not the local London-speech.[1] This came to be felt more and more to be 'dialect', i. e. to have the same sort of stamp as the country dialects of Somersetshire or Lincolnshire. Thanks to the intercourse of all these many individuals London speech gained a new smoothness which was assisted by the fact that, as London lay close to the Midlands, its speech was understood both by

---

[1] My point of view differs therefore from Wyld's who in his *Hist. of Mod. Coll. Engl.* p. 4 f. writes: 'Where does Received Standard English come from? . . . It is evident that any form of language, whatever may be its subsequent history, must in the beginning have had a local habitation . . . In other words, if Received Standard is now a Class Dialect . . . it must once have been a Regional Dialect . . . . London speech, then, or one type of it, as it existed in the fourteenth century, is the ancestor of Literary English, and it is also the ancestor of our present-day Received Standard'. According to my view a Received Standard began to be developed at the moment when people from different districts meeting together began to adapt their speech to that of the rest. This took place most of all in London, but it might also take place in other towns in which men met one another, especially in the University towns, Oxford and Cambridge. There is therefore some truth in Dibelius's view ('John Capgrave u. die engl. Schriftsprache', *Anglia* XXIII, XXIV, 1901) that Oxford contributed to the English Common Language, though he is thinking more than I am of local Oxford speech.

Northerners and by Southerners who had difficulty in understanding one another. This was asserted as early as 1387 in Higden's *Polychronicon*.[1] The chief thing is that in Standard English local peculiarities have been effaced or dropped. It is easy to collect a number of statements that the best English is the English of London, but on closer examination we shall find it recognized that the purely local element is not the decisive one. It is so even with Puttenham who declares in well-known words *(Art of Engl. Poesie* 1589. Arber's Reprint p. 156): 'Ye shall therefore take the vsual speach of the Court, and that of London and the shires lying about London within lx. miles, and not much aboue', but who side by side with this says: 'he shall follow generally the better brought vp sort . . . I say not this but that in every shyre of England there be gentlemen and others that speake but specially write as good Southerne as we of Middlesex or Surrey do'. For a later time I can quote Ellis (EEP V p. 236): 'The habit of speech among the educated classes in London may be looked upon as the basis of received speech and pronunciation'. But, in the first volume of the same work (p. 23), he says: 'In the present day we may recognize a received pronunciation all over the country, not widely differing in any particular locality, and admitting a certain degree of variety. It may be especially considered as the educated pronunciation of the metropolis, of the Court, the pulpit, and the bar.'

---

[1] 'Inde est quod Mercii sive Mediterranei Angli, tamquam participantes naturam extremorum, collaterales linguas arcticam et antarcticam melius intelligant quam adinvicem se intelligunt jam extremi'.

Sweet (*Primer of Spoken Englisn*, 1890) speaks of 'the educated speech of London and the district round it — the original home of Standard English both in its spoken and literary form. That literary English is the London dialect pure and simple, has now been proved beyond a doubt by the investigations of the German, Morsbach . . . . . I having expressed the same view in the same year in my *History of English Sounds*' But in a later work (*Sounds of English* 1908) he says: 'The best speakers of Standard English are those whose pronunciation, and language generally, least betray their locality'. This is really the point of view which I had expressed as early as 1890 (see above, p. 46).

We see a somewhat similar evolution of a standard language in France. According to Vossler the language of Old French literary works never had an exclusively *local* colour, the writer's social position and calling having a greater influence on his handling of language than his place of origin. Later, 'French', i. e. the language of the Ile de France with Paris as its centre, comes to the front. But this is not in a positive sense the dialect of that district or that city, but even in the 11th and 12th centuries is described negatively as not-Norman, not-Champagne etc.: so that there is only 'an ideal, a norm towards which one steers from different homes of dialect; but an ideal not to be attained at once from any dialect, not even the most central of them; an ideal which indeed gravitates towards a geographical or, it may be, cultural centre, but need not have originated there' (*Litbl*. 1917, p. 110, further developed in FK). Thurot has collected dicta

of the early French grammarians on the subject of
the best French.[1] Most of them name Paris as the
home of the finest French, but side by side with this,
the Court is often mentioned, or the higher Courts of
Justice, and of course not seldom the educated classes or the higher classes ('les honnetes gens de la
capitale' or 'la bonne compagnie'). But we find suggestions which go in the opposite direction. Fabri in
1521 speaks of a pronunciation which soars above
barbarous dialects, Palsgrave in 1530 declares that a
functionary of the government, wherever he dwells, can
talk French perfectly, and Hindret in 1687 lays stress
upon the Court as the place where leading personages
from the provinces who talk a purer French than others
from the same district come together and polish and
correct ('rectifient et polissent') each other's speech
while they consort with the King's own entourage.

In Germany there will not be so many voices raised
in favour of considering the speech of the capital as
determining that of the whole country. This is natural
It is only since 1871 that Berlin has counted as the
capital of all Germany, and even so it has never been
the capital of that part of the German-speaking territory
which belongs to Austria. Such voices however are
heard[2] and apart from them we hear utterances which

[1] *La Prononciation français*. Paris 1881, I p lxxxvii ff. Cp.
also Koschwitz, *Les Parlers parisiens*, Paris, 1893, preface.

[2] 'That the language of cultivated Berliners is the model
German which we hear so much about is to us in Berlin an obvious fact, against which all protests of the local patriots and dia-
lect-lovers of Middle, South, and West Germany can avail nothing'
Tanger, *Herrigs Archiv* LXXXIX p. 75 (1892).

show that the language of Berlin is spreading outside its natural sphere. [1]

But there will be many more to maintain that the best German pronunciation is that of the educated class in North Germany, and in favour of this view will advance the argument that by the recognition of this fact a compromise is arrived at, South Germany contributing the High German form of the word, and North Germany that of the sound; so that this 'High German in Low German mouth' is comparable with the famous Italian 'lingua toscana in bocca romana'.

In both these formulations I see a partial recognition of the principle of compromise with softening of strictly local peculiarities. But this softening has taken place to a greater degree in North Germany than in the much sub-divided South-Germany where every town and district has to a greater extent got the right of talking 'wie ihm der Schnabel gewachsen ist' ('as it pleases'). Other factors in Germany (the influence of actors, officials, military service) have already been discussed

In Finland until modern times the only literary language known was the foreign language, Swedish, used by the upper classes, the Finnish language spoken by the mass of the people being looked down upon as a vulgar jargon. When at the beginning of the 19th century Finnish acquired a better standing, writers at

----

[1] 'Is not the Berlin pronunciation of 'j' for 'g' steadily („im militärschritt") making its way far and wide into Middle Germany?' Schuchardt, *Über die Lautgesetze*, 1885, p. 15. 'I have before now heard Suabian officers talking in Berlin dialect'. Rambeau, *Engl Studien* XV p. 386 (1891).

first employed in the main the dialect of Åbo, the ecclesiastical capital. Later, forms and words from other districts came more and more into use, so that the language lost much of its merely local character, and could more and more be described as common to the whole country (Setälä, *Sprachrichtigkeit* p. 50 f.).

*

I can now close this survey of the different factors which have co-operated to create and diffuse a Standard Language in place of locally-coloured rustic dialects. It is important, as I think, to see that we have not to do with some single determining cause, but with many forces at play at the same time. Our intellectual life is extraordinarily complex and its most potent instrument, language, is also extraordinarily complex in consequence. The conditions of its evolution cannot be reduced to a single definite formula, unless we are content with the one formula that covers everything, Standard Languages are *socially* determined.

It is also worth while to insist strongly on the fact that the various forces which contributed in earlier times to produce and preserve linguistic unity were never since the world began so strong as they were in the last half of the nineteenth century and as they are now in the twentieth century One may mention great political unifications, and be it observed, unifications on the lines of nationality; greater mutual intercourse owing to the vast development of the means of communication — railways, tramways, motors, steamships, telephones, wireless etc., cheap books and newspapers in the interest of literary communism — finally the enormous growth of many great cities which attract a population from outside. [1] Some of these forces have not been perhaps of unqualified benefit to humanity, but of the colossal influence they have each had and still have in assisting tendencies to linguistic unity and counteracting tendencies to linguistic subdivision, there cannot be a shadow of doubt. So far as it is humanly possible to discern, one dare prophesy that unless something quite incalculable happens which completely changes the way of life on this globe, the future will see greater and greater unifications in all languages which are spoken essentially in the same way by millions of speakers. [2]

[1] 'When M. Germiquet (born in 1820) came to live at Sorvillier (Berne) he and his family were the only people there who spoke (Standard) French. In 1896 there were only a few old people left to talk the local dialect. One must say that the nineteenth century witnessed a complete linguistic change in France, the transition from local idioms to common French. The country people have changed speech as well as costume; there is an enormous difference between things as I saw them half a century ago and as I see them now'. (Meillet, BSL XXII. 228). The same change has been seen in the same period in many countries besides France.

[2] H. C. Wyld (*Hist. Mod. Coll. Eng.* p. 7) thinks that the process of differentiation is almost infinite, and the tendency of language is not, as it has sometimes been wrongly said, in the direction of uniformity, but of variety. The former view, which arose from a realization that the old Regional Dialects of England were disappearing, lost sight of the fact that their place was being taken by a totally different form of English, not developed normally from the several Regional Dialects, but one of different origin, acquired through external channels. The old dialects were not growing like each other, but were vanishing. In their places various forms of Modified Standard have arisen.

Meanwhile, complete agreement is never attained. The circumstances are too complex. Even people with an excellent mastery of the Common Language will among the thousands and thousands of details which go to make up a language keep some feature or other of the local dialect of their place of origin. Some even, even though they belong to the best educated classes, feel a certain pride in retaining traces of their native district, and with a certain coquetry flaunt before our eyes some of the most noticeable features of its dialect. (I have observed this in some of my colleagues — professors of the University of Copenhagen — and in some Danish politicians, either now living or recently deceased). But this is something quite different from really speaking the dialect of the district, which they, and perhaps other people, fancy they are doing.

It is also no rare thing that a man who day by day in peaceful circumstances speaks the Standard Language irreproachably, may in moments of passion slip back into the dialect of his childhood, — a trait of human nature which is sometimes introduced by novelists with great effect. [1]

His view seems to rest on his thinking of dialects as existing independently of the people who speak them. It is still however a fact that these 'various forms of Modified Standard' are more like one another than were the old geographical dialects, and so there has been a movement of approximation, not one of divergence. And this has been due simply to modern social developments, which are at least as 'normal' as they would have been if the old districts had remained severally isolated and the dialects had been able to split up even more than they did under medieval or pre-medieval conditions.

[1] ' "Ye donnard auld devil", answered Monkbarns, his Scottish accent predominating when in anger, though otherwise not

If the views here presented are accepted, the Standard Language may be compared with the composite photographs which Galton was the first to think of and to apply to a scientific purpose. If you photograph a number of people (of the same or similar race) one over another on the same plate, you get a picture in which all small divergences from the normal vanish, and the type is shown in its purity Portraits thus produced are strikingly handsome. In the same way language perfectly purged of dialect becomes a sort of ideal language, to which real language can only approximate.

*

It may be interesting to raise the question of the value of that linguistic unification shown in the rise of a common or Standard Language. By value we mean value for the individual, for one who uses the common language instead of the special dialect of a parish or country town. We cannot dismiss the question, as some writers do, by saying that it is idle to ask whether the Standard-language or the dialect is best, just as it is idle to ask whether German or

particularly remarkable'. (Scott, *The Antiquary*). 'So furious was he that he could hardly articulate, and when he did speak, it was in a much broader and more Western dialect than any which we had heard from him in the morning' (Conan Doyle, *Baskerville's Hound* p. 72). 'When she was excited, the Harvie words came back to her, as they came back to me' (Barrie, *The Little Minister*, p. 15). ' „Volé! Je suis volé . . . ma femme m'a volé pour son fils' . . et son furieux délire roulait pêle-mêle avec des jurons paysans de sa montagne: „Ah, le garso . . Ah, li bougri." ' So in Alphonse Daudet's *L'Immortel* speaks the old academician Astier-Réhu, who otherwise talks elegant Standard French.

French is best. I would answer the last question by saying that in Germany German is best, and in France, French, if one would make sure of being understood But the question of Standard Language *versus* Dialect is not on the same footing, because in the same country, in Denmark or England, we make a choice between the two when we address the same people. It is thus seen that so far from the question being an idle one, it is on the contrary of the greatest importance to every single person who has the choice to make — unless circumstances have made the choice for him, through his having been educated and having lived in such a way that he has only one of these forms of speech at his command.

The value of a Common Language for the whole country is therefore something which has been felt strongly in many places by many different people, most of all naturally by writers desirous of reaching a wide circle of readers. And where such a Common Language has not yet become an actuality, advanced minds feel the great inconveniences that come from the want of it and in some cases have consciously worked to bring a single language into existence.

Brunot (cp. Vossler FK p. 186) quotes the complaint of a Lorrainer at the beginning of the Middle French period that the language was so corrupted that people could hardly understand each other, one man talking and writing in one fashion, and another in another. We have also a well known utterance [1] of Caxton when he was introducing the art of printing into England at the end of the 15th century. He, more than other people,

---

[1] Printed e. g. GS. § 69.

felt the inconveniences of dialects, as he naturally wished to print books that would be read by all who spoke English at that date. But, says he, what form is one to use when people in the north say 'egg' while in the south they only understand 'ey'? A choice in this case had to be made, and it may be said at once that Caxton on the whole made a sensible choice in harmony with the tendencies to unity which had made themselves felt even before his time, and with a premonition of the direction these tendencies would take in the future. His language more than that of many contemporary writers agrees with later Standard English.

*

In the above mentioned definition of a Standard Language as the language of those speakers by whose pronunciation one cannot hear from what district they come, there is really nothing said of the value of such a language.

The definition merely shows us how to recognize it. But if we carry the implied thought further and say: the language which has freed itself from everything in the speech of a single district which hinders one or makes it difficult for one to be understood by people from another district, we get at once an indication of value. The Standard Language strikes no one as odd, and so opens the door to understanding in wider circles than does the country dialect. If I am talking to one or two people, I can make myself understood best if I talk their own speech, but if I do not know their particular dialect, I succeed best by using the Standard Language. For every part of the country that comes *second*-best. And if I am addressing many people at once, say in a meeting of people from many different districts, then without the least doubt it is the Common Language which will convey my thoughts best and most surely to the minds of all. The same thing holds if, when I write, I am addressing a circle of readers whose extent and composition I do not know nor can see at a glance. Here we get the meaning and at the same time the natural explanation of the statement that the evolution of a Common Language goes side by side with the evolution of a national literature. Nowadays no one can dispense with the written language: it is known, or needs to be known, by all. The question of the value of the Common Language becomes therefore identical with the question whether it is better that the Standard Language should be a foreign language to everyone, or everyone's most natural means of expression.

Those who cling to the keeping up of dialects will reply that we ought not to aim at a colourless uniformity, and that there is great value in the variety which allows every district to keep its own peculiar characteristics. But we may retort, that even if differences of speech between one district and another are effaced, we are not reduced to a dead monotony. Within the domain of the Standard Language there is room for great individual differences: think of such marked personalities as Søren Kierkegaard and H. C. Andersen, or in England of Tennyson and Browning, who wrote 'the same language' at the same time, and yet how differently! And it is to be observed that these differences are perhaps quite as valuable to mankind as the differences between the Devonshire and Yorkshire dialects. The dialects certainly have their beauty, but much of their picturesqueness can be taken over, and, indeed, is being taken over into the common language. On the other hand we cannot say that everything in rustic dialects is valuable or attractive. The unspoilt, uncorrupted, natural speech of peasants has its own beauty and it is certainly prettier than the mixed speech they often come out with when they wish to be genteel and are not entirely masters of genteel language. Changes are always costly, — the parents scarcely ever succeed in talking the Standard Language quite naturally, but the children can attain to it. And this is to their advantage, not merely materially, because they can more easily, obtain positions in society which now — whether one approves it or not in the abstract — are given by preference to people whose speech is free from dialect, but also because they thus escape being looked down on on account of their speech and are therefore saved from many unpleasant humiliations. Apart from all this, merely by reason of their way of speaking they have a better chance of coming in contact with others and getting a fuller interchange of ideas. Nowadays even peasants in remote districts come in touch with many more people from other parts of the country than was the case in earlier times. If a peasant has many oddities of speech, these are a bar to the simplest exchange of thoughts between him and anyone who talks the Standard Language or the dialect of a different district, so that all real conversation is at a standstill, and he is restricted to the most necessary remarks or to some trivial sentences. That is why the townsman considers the countryman stupider and more destitute of ideas than he really is, and *vice versâ*, and so the difference in language begets a mutual disdain and class-prejudice.

If the dialects are to be preserved by the side of the Common Language, it means that many will in fact be compelled to learn two languages, and those just of the class which is in other ways worst off and has least time for schooling. It will be more valuable for them to come into constant and comprehensive touch with the Standard Language. They then acquire only one language and get a greater mastery of it.

Lastly it must be remembered that dialect is less able to express the higher interests of the mind: people whose minds are awake and developed cannot be confined to a dialect. The Common-speech is in itself richer in colour and opens wider vistas and there is plenty of room in it for that picturesque variety which in the opinion of many people can only be retained by the preservation of dialects. If we think out logically and bravely what is for the good of society, our view of language will lead us to the conclusion that it is our duty to work in the direction which natural evolution has already taken, i. e. towards the diffusion of the common language at the cost of local dialects.

This implies no contempt for dialects or for those who use them. An investigator of the laws of language will naturally be much interested in the study of country ways of speech as they may often yield him valuable hints which he could not get from the study of literary languages. Philologists often say that the study of dialect is more important than the study of Standard Languages. One often sees the reason given (e. g. by Setälä, *Sprachricht.* p. 53) that the phenomena of dialects are simpler, and so in them it is easier for investigators to find general laws. But the laws thus found may be only of limited validity. No side of language can be neglected by investigators, but there are plenty of sides to investigate, especially syntax, style, semantics, in which the literary languages present matters of greater interest to investigators than any dialect. If the study of dialect has hitherto played so great a part in investigation it has been largely because the more psychological sides of language have been somewhat neglected, and nearly exclusive attention given to sounds and forms. At any rate in appraising the two kinds of language we must not take account of the interests of the investigator when a gain to him means a loss to the user of the language. Here the answer cannot be doubtful.

I must close this chapter with a reference to a fact which has been already touched, viz. that along with the evolution of the greater communities comes a certain heterogeneity in the individuals who speak 'the same language'. There is greater homogeneity as regards language between the members of a little tribe — perhaps only a few hundreds, — than between the 150,000,000 more or less who form the English-speaking community. Connected with this is a fact which has been emphasized by Fouillée and after him by van Ginneken *(Anthropos II* p. 704) and which extends to

other things besides language, namely that the more
primitive a people is, the more likeness one finds
between individuals of the same tribe, and the less
likeness between one tribe and another. Conversely,
the more civilized a people is, the greater is the
unlikeness between different individuals, and the more
striking are the points of likeness between the one
people and another. Civilization furthers individual
differentiation, while uncultivated people are completely
dependent on their *milieu* and tied to the traditional
way of thinking.

CHAPTER V

STANDARDS OF CORRECTNESS

The individual in his use of the language has constantly to improvise. He continually finds himself in new situations and has things to express which he has never before met in exactly the same shape.

He is like a chess-player who at every move is faced with a position of the pieces which he has never seen, but who makes his move much as he has done before in similar positions. Or he is like a pianist who sits down to the piano to play a fantasia, and who more or less consciously has recourse to a number of motifs heard on some previous occasion, musical commonplaces, scraps of melody, and well-worn harmonies, so that much that he plays is well-known, and even what is new is largely invented after an old pattern. But the person who plays in this sort of way on a language is in one way in a different position to a man improvising on a musical instrument. He aims at being understood He is accordingly obliged to accommodate himself to the prepossessions of his listeners. A norm is set before him which he cannot disregard with impunity. And so we are brought to the question of correct speaking. What amount of liberty can an individual allow himself?

Questions of correctness of speech crop up constantly in all countries. They play a great part in school-teaching. But one whose schooldays are over is still often faced with the question, if this or that word, this or that spelling, this or that pronunciation, is 'right' He may waver between two forms, two words, two expressions, and would like to know which is to be preferred.

Such questions are often discussed in the newspapers or in special dissertations — as, for example, quite recently, a discussion arose whether the country in which we are at present ought rightly to be called 'Norge' or 'Noreg'. [1]

I need hardly say that I cannot here discuss a number of particular cases in any particular language. But it falls within my province to say something of the great general principles involved. On what grounds is one form deemed more correct than another? And, in cases of doubt, what is it that must decide?

Among recent philologists Adolf Noreen has treated these questions with most thoroughness. His dissertation is well-known, and has been several times reprinted, last of all in *Spridda Studier* (1895). His views have been criticized to some extent by Flodström (*Nystavaren* I p. 141 ff.), by A. Johannson in the

---

[1] So, fifty years ago, some Swedes, among them V. Rydberg, wished to substitute 'Sverike' for 'Sverige' because the form with g was looked on as due to Danish influence, while philologists nowadays hold that this g has developed quite naturally in accordance with the sound-laws of *Swedish*.

appendices to his translation of Noreen's dissertation (I F. I) and by E. Setälä (*Språkriktighet*, in *Finnisch-ugrische forschungen* IV). All three however are in fairly close agreement with Noreen's main points. According to Noreen there are three main views as to correctness in speech, two which have played the chief rôle in the Science of Language but which he rejects, and finally his own. The names he gives to these three views are the literary-historical, the natural-historical, and the rational. According to the first view the criterion of correctness is essentially agreement with the usage found in writers of an older period, which last may be very arbitrarily selected. Setälä is right however in saying that Noreen does not give a very correct account of the views advocated in Germany by Grimm, and in other countries by Grimm's disciples, in Sweden particularly by Rydqvist, the men, that is, who according to Noreen are the chief representatives of the so-called literary-historical view. It is not the case that these men, as Noreen says, wished to force the language back to an old standpoint They extolled whatever had developed regularly from the language of the earlier period in accordance with what they called the laws of the language. By this they especially meant the sound-laws, since what we now call analogy-formations were not then recognized as a justifiable factor in linguistic evolution. Setälä would therefore prefer to call their standpoint the 'grammatical': it would be still better to say the 'linguistic-historical'.

In any case, much of what Noreen says against this view is fully justified. One does not see why the particular period of linguistic history which the writers

in question took as their starting-point should be preferred to any other. There is further no reason why
people in these days should be governed by what
people said at some earlier time. Finally, the laws
which grammarians formulate are after all only human
inventions, and in many cases it appears that they can
be interpreted in different ways, and that the laws which
one generation of investigators sets up are repealed
or amended by the next. Accordingly after the sound
criticism to which it has been subjected by Noreen and
Setälä, little is left of the first view of correct speech,
even though the latter writer does not utterly reject it.

The second view, called by Noreen the natural-
historical, is based on the doctrine prevalent in a certain period of the nineteenth century that language is
an organism which will develop best in a state of
complete freedom, so that all dogmatizing or meddling
with language is an evil. The view — more or less
veiled — is still held by many philologists, who are
therefore inclined to put aside the layman's question
'What is right?' as something with which linguistic
science has no concern. 'Anarchic' would be a more
trenchant name for this view than 'natural-historical'.

Taken strictly, according to this doctrine, there can
be no right or wrong in language at all. But Noreen
says that the view cannot be pursued into its consequences without landing us in utter absurdity.

For Noreen, only one standpoint remains, Noreen's
own. He calls it — with a partiality easy to understand, as he acknowledges — the rational or common-
sense standpoint. It is really an opportunist standpoint. It debouches in the formula: 'The best is that

which can be caught most exactly and most quickly
by the audience present and be most easily produced
by the speaker', — but he accepts Flodström's altered
wording: 'The best is the speech-form which with the
necessary intelligibility unites the greatest possible sim-
plicity'. As Noreen has acknowledged, the view is
really already given in Es. Tegnér's earlier formula [1].
'That which, easiliest uttered, is easiliest understood' [2],
a formula which, according to Noreen's own definition,
deserves to be preferred before his own, since the
latter by most people will hardly be caught so exactly
and so quickly as Tegnér's.

We have therefore to do with a standard of expediency, or, as I have called it in another connexion,
a case of 'energetics': it turns on economy of effort
(or of the expenditure of energy) both on the part of
the producer and of the recipient. Setälä holds that
there is some truth in the two standpoints first mentioned, and that Noreen's standard of expediency has
therefore only a partial justification, as it does not actually decide the question whether a form is right or
wrong, but only decides whether or not it is serviceable.
Distinctions may be imagined which in themselves it
would be convenient for the language to possess, but
if they are not found in it, it would be a wrong use
of language to introduce them. Usage is therefore the
highest tribunal: it is this that decides whether something is, or is not, correct: it is only secondarily that
the question arises whether something is, or is not,

[1] In 'Språk och nationalitet' (1874), reprinted in 'Ur språkets
värld' (1922) p. 137.

[2] 'Det som lättast givet lättast förstås'.

convenient or expedient, a question which really only arises when usage in wavering. It seems to me, however, that Setälä is here taking the concept 'expedient' in a too narrow sense, since to be in agreement with general linguistic usage is in itself 'expedient'. We may therefore with equal justice reverse his position and say that expediency is the supreme principle, and it is that which dictates that we must accommodate ourselves to what is now the established usage of the language we speak.

I may be permitted to mention some points in which I think that Noreen is fairly open to criticism. He considers (p. 163) that it is an unqualified advantage to a language to have as many synonyms (i. e. expressions of nearly the same meaning) as possible, and says that a language in which every shade of thought has its particular expression is unfortunately a Utopia. In saying this, he has not considered what is implied in 'every shade of thought'. Should there be particular expressions for every *nuance* of colour distinguishable by the eye? Should we have innumerable words instead of the three 'hillock', 'hill', 'mountain'? Should we besides 'hot', 'cold', 'lukewarm', have a multitude of expressions for different degrees of heat? Noreen is, of course, right in saying that a language with an expression for every *nuance* of human thought is an impossibility. But we cannot sympathize with him in his considering this unfortunate, and in calling such an imaginary language a Utopia, something in itself to be desired. As I think, it would be simply a linguistic Hell.

Language is only attending to its proper business when it comprehends a multitude of like things under

the same appellation[1]: it is just this which makes the
communication of thought possible. Synonyms are all
very well, but only within reasonable bounds. One
has to remember (what Noreen here clearly forgets)
that words are not obtained without cost. Every word
that is to be used or understood must be first learnt.
We have therefore to weigh against one another the
advantage of having accurately shaded expressions, and
the inconvenience of learning and remembering them.
English has a great number of synonyms, because,
especially in the last four centuries, it has taken over a
mass of words from the classical languages. But this is
by no means an unqualified blessing, as I have tried
to point out in my *Growth and Structure of the English Language*.

Noreen attaches great weight to 'the relativity' of
his formula, in that it takes account of the audience
of the moment. An expression, e. g. a foreign word,
which may be the best when one is addressing an
educated audience, may be bad, or completely inadmis-
sible, when one is addressing people who are not qual-
ified to understand it. There is, of course, something right in this view. But it overlooks the fact that
it is by no means convenient to the speaker to have
to submit too much to weighing his words according
to the more or less casual audience he has before him
at the moment. Often, for example, when a man is
writing a book, he does not know in the least into
whose hands it will fall, and it is impossible to adapt
himself to their needs. If we are to decide what is
desirable in a language, we must from the standpoint

[1] Cp. *Philos. of Grammar*, p. 63 ff.

of 'energetics' prefer the state of things in which the same form, the same word can be used to all speakers of the language whatsoever. Then it will not be necessary to consider at every moment whether one's expression falls within the mental horizon of the person addressed, or is far over his head. In taking this position, we are laying stress on the unifying function of language as a bond between all the members of a community; that is, on its national as opposed to its individual side.

Noreen's strong insistence on regard to the audience of the moment, if pursued to its logical conclusion, lands us in strange consequences. Imagine, for example, a highly educated Frenchman speaking some sentences in his most irreproachable French to a Norwegian peasant. According to Noreen's definition, his language is utterly incorrect. But would it not be more reasonable to define 'correct speech' in such a manner that we could say that in the given circumstances the Frenchman was talking correctly (talking correct French), but that it was incorrect (inexpedient) of him to talk French to the Norwegian peasant? The question of 'correct speech' can only arise *within* a given language.

The same perversity is shown in another way. When Noreen says 'what is not understood is incorrect' thinking all the while of the audience of the moment, his words presuppose that the want of understanding is always due to the speaker, and is to be laid to his charge.

But if the cause lies in the extraordinary stupidity of the hearer and his not understanding what ordinary people would take in easily, is the language used therefore 'incorrect'? Noreen illustrates his remark (p. 163) by saying that foreign words like 'timid' and 'nonchalant' are 'obviously wrong' in purely popular writing addressed to the Swedish people. But he takes no account of the fact that a word, otherwise not understood, can often be made intelligible by the context, and that this is the way in which all of us in our childhood, and to a less degree in after years, widen our vocabulary. A discreet use of foreign words or technical expressions may then, even in 'halfpenny rags for the people', be a factor in healthy movements of popular education.

The Tegnér-Noreen-Flodström formula postulates that regard should be had both to the speaker and to the hearer. It gives us therefore two standards of value without indicating in any way how it is to be decided which of the two considerations is the more important. That there can arise a conflict between the two parties has been specially emphasized by Flodström. The more lightly the speaker takes his task, the more slovenly he is in fact (it may be in pronunciation, it may also be in his choice of words and the arrangement of his thoughts), the more difficult is it for the hearer to understand him. Clearly Noreen will give most consideration to the recipient. But it is not easy to see why the hearer is to be favoured at the cost of the speaker. The two ought to have equal rights just like the two parties to a bargain. In many cases it is evidently a question of more or less, but let us suppose a case in which the hearer vaguely seizes the speaker's meaning when he expresses himself in the way customary in his own circle, in the way easiest to

himself, that is; while in order to secure that his audience of the moment should understand him to the
absolutely fullest extent, he would be compelled to exert
himself to an extraordinary degree. Would it not be
unreasonable to make this extreme demand of him?

On the other hand, it may be urged (see my *Fonetik* p. 114 ff.) that, if we look more deeply into the
matter, there need not always be any conflict of interests between the two parties. It is to the speaker's
interest to ensure that he is understood as exactly as
possible. He speaks in order to produce an impression, not to slip out of his task on the easiest terms.
We are getting perhaps to the heart of the question
when we observe that there is something which speaker
and hearer have in common, and that this common
element really makes many things easy for both of
them. This is the linguistic norm which they have
both accepted from without, from the community, from
society, from the nation. When all is said, the correctness of their speech, even for themselves, is not determined by the particular relation to each other of the
two persons talking at the moment, the two individuals,
Jack and Jill, who are having a chat. They talk and
understand one another in virtue of both belonging to
the same linguistic community. And in 999 cases out
of a thousand, it is this Community, and not any special consideration of what would be expedient at that
chance moment, that, even for them, determines what
is linguistically correct in what they say to one another.
Noreen's formula is too individualistic, too atomistic, it
breaks up the linguistic community too much into particular individuals, it takes too little account of the whole.

One may further object to Noreen that he at once propounds the question, what *ought* to be the deciding factor, -while he would have gone deeper if he had first inquired what as a matter of fact does decide, or has decided, questions of this kind. When the question is raised if this or that is correct or not, the layman in almost every case has his verdict ready to hand. But it is just as indisputable that as a rule he will not advance *either* of the two views which according to Noreen have hitherto been supreme, namely the so-called literary-historical and the natural-historical. These views have possibly played a great part in the purely theoretical deliberations of linguistic investigators (more properly, only of linguistic historians). But in practice, in the discussion of questions of this kind in class-rooms, in newspapers and in daily conversation, the appeal is made to quite different things than these. What is the ordinary man going on when he gives his opinion whether this or that expression is correct or not? We cannot expect him to have any set system, he will now appeal to one thing and now to another, and to the average man it matters nothing that the standard he advances today for the decision of some question may conflict with that which he considered decisive of another difficulty yesterday. But certainly the list that follows includes the most important of his standards,

(1) the standard of authority,
(2) the geographical standard.
(3) the literary standard,
(4) the aristocratic standard,
(5) the democratic standard,

(6) the logical standard,

(7) the æsthetic standard.

Let us take them one by one. As we go, we shall here and there have an opportunity to turn back to the views set forth by Noreen.

*

(1) In some countries the Ministry of Education concerns itself with linguistic questions and issues decisions (especially on questions of orthography), which the schools controlled by the ministry are bound to accept. From the schools the influence spreads further, so that what is enjoined by the ministry comes to be considered as binding on the whole community. In other countries there are Academies (of which the French Academy is the most famous) which are appealed to as the supreme authority to decide linguistic questions, an authority to which all submit, or did submit formerly. Meanwhile it is clear that an external authority of this kind is not in itself sovereign. There will always be independent spirits who will set themselves in opposition to its decisions, or, at least, cavil at them, and strive to get the authority to alter its decrees in this point or that. Further neither the ministry nor the Academy settles every doubtful point. There will always be points on which one cannot get, or has not got, their decision, especially when new conceptions and new words have cropped up. Here, even among the Ministry's advisers or in the Academy itself, there may be some discussion as to what is to be preferred, and while they are deliberating, indeed right up to the time, when their judgment is pro-

nounced, it is clearly of no use to point to the Ministry or to the Academy as the supreme authority. There must then be a something still higher, and consequently in principle reference to the external authority decides nothing.

It is shown by the case of England that there is no need for any such official or semi-official authority. Englishmen have never been inclined to have an Academy, like the French Academy, founded to formulate rules for their language or its orthography, and no English Ministry has interfered in any questions of this kind. And still there are a multitude of things in English which must be said to be generally established as correct speech, even as the only correct speech, while on the other hand there are a vast multitude of things which Englishmen consider incorrect and avoid just as rigorously as the French avoid what is stamped as incorrect by their Academy.

Meanwhile it is characteristic of human nature that most people wish for an external authority, even in linguistic questions. Just as they uncritically adapt themselves to much of what their tailors or their newspapers tell them about the particular cut of clothes which 'people' are wearing at the moment, so they wish to have some definite direction as to the pronunciation, spelling and use of words. If they have not a teacher at hand who can give them an infallible rule to settle their doubts, they rely blindly on the dictionary or grammar which they happen to have. Very naturally, for it is obviously not everyone's business to go deeply into the question why this or that usage is to be preferred.

Now and then some one writer may come to be regarded and consulted as authoritative, when perhaps it never entered his head to pose as anything of the sort. Vaugelas and his contemporaries had no desire to be anything else than observers of the best linguistic usage of society, and never gave themselves out as legislators in regard to the language. Yet such were they considered in their own time and largely also in after times. It is just the same with the best dictionaries in different countries, even with the French Academy itself. The latter says expressly that it does not consider itself as lord of the French language, but only desires to find out and fix what the usage (or the usage of the best writers) actually is. In every successive edition, therefore, it admits the neologisms which have found favour since the last edition was published, without regard to any opinion which members of the Academy may personally entertain as to the value of these neologisms. That at any rate is the theoretical position. But this does not prevent the great majority of Frenchmen from looking on the Academicians as the authoritative legislators of the language and, as such, entitled to unconditional obedience.

Combined with this craving to have an external authority to cling to, goes a wish on the part of the great majority to get quite definite short rules. This is met very willingly by the writers of the usual grammatical textbooks, who are themselves inclined to imprison the language in set rules. The rules are based very frequently on a correct observation of the actual language used in certain circumstances, which is then (incorrectly) generalized, the rules being then considered to apply to all cases without exception. Many grammarians of the ordinary type are also disposed to make small, subtle distinctions, which they expect to be observed, even though they are of no practical value for the understanding of the language or for clearness of thought, and are therefore merely a burden to those who use the language.

It is largely against such rules as these, sometimes too general, sometimes too special, and lacking any real basis in the language, as well as against too great rigidity in the use of language that linguistic historians feel themselves called upon to protest.

Anyone, who has studied with any thoroughness the earlier forms of the language and compared them with those of his own day, will have had his eyes opened to the great mutability of the language. He will therefore ever insist that what is 'right' in one century, is 'wrong' in the next, and that language develops by constantly breaking away from what was required previously. It is therefore not surprising that many linguistic historians have no interest in questions of 'correct speech', and well nigh consider it beneath their dignity as men of science to concern themselves with them. Thy feel tempted to say with Shelley:

> Man's yesterday may ne'er be like his morrow:
> Nought may endure but Mutability.

In taking this attitude however the linguistic historian may easily come to tip out the baby along with the bathwater. Even though the language changes century by century, and even though it is found that the new element which enters the language in the course of its changes often turns out to be of more value than the old, there is still no need to put aside the question of 'correct speech'. We ought to be able to see that it is still an important question for every generation whether it should say this or that, whether this or that form is correct, and so on, and that it would be regrettable if those who were most competent to decide such questions should leave the decision to the less competent. The linguistic historian will be able to look on these questions from a higher standpoint, and to bring a greater number of important considerations into the discussion. He will have no inclination to confine the language in too strait rules, but will bear in mind that what seems capricious in it may be deeply rooted in its whole structure, if all the forces in the complex game are to have full play. He will therefore have more feeling than the average schoolmaster for the natural movements of the language and will blame the pedant for requiring in English the stiff 'To whom are you talking?'. He knows that for three centuries the only natural thing for Englishmen to say has been 'Who are you talking to?'. And so in many other cases.

*

(2) The question is often put in this form, Where in Denmark (or England) do they speak the best Danish (or English)? The reply is often, in some particular town, generally the capital, but sometimes a smaller town, Roskilde or Oxford — or a particular district as Poitou for French. But after what has been said of the non-local common-language, we shall not be satisfied with this purely local or geographical defini-

tion. Not everything that is heard in the selected place is linguistically correct, and one may often hear the language faultlessly spoken elsewhere.

What might be called a negatively geographical attitude has been very characteristically emphasized in Harold Palmer's new and able book *A Grammar of Spoken English*[1]. The whole of his discussion leads us to what Noreen called the natural-historical view, which is said to have been expressed by a number of well-known philologists, among whom I am wrongly given a place. Palmer speaks of 'the persistence of that age-long series of enquiries "where is English best spoken?" "In what part of France do they speak the most correct French?", "Where is purest German found?" etc., etc. The mere use in this connexion of such terms as "best" or "correct" implies that there is in the mind of the enquirer an implicit belief in the existence of some standard- or super-dialect, the superiority or intrinsic "correctness" of which cannot be questioned. The only possible answers to such questions are "The best Scottish-English is spoken in Scotland", "The best American-English is spoken in the United States", "The purest London-English is to be found in London" .... "The only pure form for Slocum-in-the-Hole-English is used at the village of Slocum-in-the-Hole".... There is no Real, Genuine, or Pure English, French, etc., and there never has been. But the chimerical idea of a standard dialect still persists. In vain do the most eminent and most respected linguistic authorities deny its existence; in vain do the most erudite grammarians and etymologists assure us that the sole standard is,

[1] Cambridge 1924, p. 32 ff.

and always has been, that of correct usage. .... No one can offend against the grammar of his own dialect. "Ain't yer comin' 'ome?" is a correct grammatical form of the Lower Cockney dialect and an incorrect grammatical form in the dialect of any present-day educated speech'.

This is as much as to say that there is a set of co-ordinate local dialects all equally right, but within each of them the question crops up again, 'What is correct?' 'What is best?' as we may see by the adjectives which Palmer himself uses, — to be sure, with the self-contradiction that lies in the words 'No one can offend against the grammar of his own dialect'. The problem is accordingly thrust aside, not solved.

*

(3). Very frequently when the question of linguistic correctness is raised, the inquirer is told that he should follow the best authors. This point of view is expressed in a rather subdued tone by Noreen, and more loudly by Setälä, who does not entirely succeed in reconciling it with his otherwise purely linguistic way of thinking. Apart from the fact that this way of considering the question does not help us the least little bit in the question of what is correct in pronunciation, — though that too belongs to the province of correct speech, — its most essential defect in my opinion is that it transfers the decision to something outside the purely linguistic domain. To discover which authors we should follow, we must make a literary valuation, and this in the absence of any generally established standard, is in itself uncertain so that opinions may differ widely. People will generally agree best about the so-called classical authors who belong to a previous age, but their language will necessarily be in many respects obsolete, so that no one will follow them out and out.

In England it will be generally agreed that Shakespeare as an author stands supreme, but no one will set up his language as a perfect model to a writer of today. His works are constantly being reprinted, but — it is worth noting — not in his own spelling, or in that of his age. Even in 1632, nine years after the first collected edition of his dramas, the Second Folio came out with the object of smoothing the irregularities in his language, and removing a good deal which people at that time did not approve as good English. At the beginning of the 18th century Pope in his edition corrected Shakespeare's language and style in countless points. Even if modern editors follow the path of sound philology by seeking to bring the text into the exactest possible agreement with what the author himself wrote, no regard being paid to the approval or disapproval of people of today, it still of course does not mean that they are setting him up as a model to be imitated unreservedly. His language, indeed, differs in so many points from Modern English, that we need notes upon it, and several Shakespeare-Dictionaries have been written to make it clear to the modern reader.

The same considerations apply to the unavoidable changes found in the languages of all countries, and again and again one will be placed in extreme difficulty by finding that where two or more authors are set up as the best, the language of one differs from that of another. Ibsen does not write like Bjørnson, and Bjørnson writes very differently at different times. A literary standard will therefore in many cases leave us in the lurch.

Further, authors are to be found here and there whose thought entitles them to a high place in literature, but whose language and style present such peculiarities that no one would set them up as models of language. But if we exclude them, and say that people should take as models, not those authors who are best in themselves, but those who write their native language best and have the best style, it is clear that from that moment the literary standard of correct language has been abandoned, while on the contrary language has become the standard by which literary writers are appraised. We set up as the best language that which is found in the best writers, and count as the best writers those that best write the language. We are therefore no further advanced than before.

It is something quite different to direct people to the great writers when a discussion has arisen on some single point of linguistic correctness. This may often be done with effect, especially when we are dealing with narrow-minded fellow-citizens who have infallible opinions on matters of this kind, and are much disposed, on the basis of preconceived ideas, to condemn this or that as utterly reprehensible on grammatical or logical grounds. These people can sometimes — but not always! — be reduced to silence when it is pointed out to them that the rejected word, or whatever it may be, is frequently found in even the very best writers. This works far better than a theoretical proof that their grammatical or logical arguments are untenable, since often their weakness can only be revealed after a thorough scientific examination. But with the initiated it is of no use to conceal the fact that references to good writers are not in themselves decisive of the question. It is no proof that an expression is correct that it is found in a great writer. Even the greatest geniuses can make mistakes, even the greatest artists in language are not always at their best, even Homer takes a nap now and then, even the sun has spots — but whether or not they *are* spots, we must decide for ourselves by means of other criteria.

We cannot however altogether reject recourse to the great writers as determining, or helping to determine, questions of linguistic correctness. One thing must especially be noticed, the range of the circle in which a man's words have an effect. While an ordinary person is only heard by two or three perhaps at a time, the author by his writings is talking at the same time to thousands, and, for that reason alone, is gaining greater influence in regard to language. It is true enough that the number of readers does not merely depend on the value of the thought. The 'short par's', of a mediocre journalist are read perhaps by more people than the finest and most thoughtful poem The greatest authors are not the 'best sellers' But the great authors have still this advantage over the others, that even if at the moment they have fewer readers, their works live longer, and are read again and again when the insects of a day are forgotten. They are more powerful in their working and contribute more puissantly than ordinary men to unity, identity and stability in language. And still their greater actual influence does not justify us in setting up their language as the supreme model of correctness.

✳

(4) What now of the definition of the best language as 'the language of the upper class'? or, as it may perhaps be expressed less offensively, 'the language of good society'? Here we encounter similar difficulties to those in the last case; for involuntarily one asks: What upper class? What good society? Where are we to draw the line and whom shall we include? Shall we go to the Court and the nobility? Then, Danes at any rate, will recall a time, when their Court and their nobility were under a strong German influence, and when the sounds and accent of Holstein were considered in the highest circles as specially refined,[1] though they were utterly un-Danish, and were not recognized as things to be imitated outside a narrow circle. We shall of course be no better off if we draw the line by income, and so reckon among those whose language is to be imitated a set of vulgar upstarts, 'gullasj-baroner', 'profiteers', as they were called in the War

Are we to say 'the leisured classes', those who are not obliged to toil for their bread? Or the higher government-servants and professional classes? The cultivated, who have enjoyed the highest education the age can give? This form of discrimination would certainly be more attractive to many people than the more external ones already mentioned. But where are we to draw the line?

[1] Cp. the Hanoverian influence at one time in the English Court.

In spite of the difficulty of defining which higher class is to be regarded, it cannot be denied that with this standard, which can be called for short the aristocratic standard, we have got hold of something that is important. Class-distinctions have actually played and are still playing an extraordinarily great part in the evolution of languages and in the popular judgment of what is right or wrong. The lower class — or part of the lower class, or, we should say perhaps, some of the lower classes — strive to a great extent to copy their 'betters', and so seek to become more refined, or at least to appear more refined, than they actually are. It is not always what is valuable in the upper class that is imitated, either in such things as clothes and outward behaviour or in language. But the imitation, or desire to imitate, is a fact: and it leads even to certain forms of speech being considered by the humble class as 'more refined' than others. In return, the upper class, which looks down on the lower class, extends its disdain to that class's language. It is hall-marked as ignorant or vulgar. But this is no purely linguistic appraisement. It is possible that an objective critic might find something or other in the vulgar speech more admirable in itself than the corresponding idiom of the higher class. There is no real consideration of the abstract value of the two forms. All that is considered is where those forms hail from, — if they go with elegant manners, fine clothes etc., or if they are found in the mouth of persons who cannot afford much every day for soap or books, and who are engaged in more or less dirty work. We may lament that men are so constituted, that class-distinctions should ever have arisen, and that these have been reflected in class-dialects, but the fact is not to be explained away or lamented away: we must take it as it is. The philologist especially who lays stress on the social side of a language, cannot get away from the aristocratic appraisement of language as a factor of importance.

There is probably no country in which the question of the correct and elegant use of language has been more discussed than France, where, especially since the 17th century, a long series of grammarians and other writers have applied themselves to it with great thoroughness. But what, in the view of these writers, are the grounds for determining whether anything belongs to 'la bonne langue', which is set up as a model? Brunot has collected and analysed their views; and Meillet in discussing[1] Brunot's book, writes: 'Even those interested in the matter have not known where this exemplary language was to be found. At the Court? But there you found people from the provinces and people who spoke badly. In writers? But the French language has not been fixed by writers, it has not been a mere literary language, it is a language of good society ("une langue de société"). An appeal is made to usage, but the particular kind of usage meant is not exactly defined. Obviously the usage of the common people is to be shunned, and we are tempted to ask whether the leading principle, to a greater degree than Brunot admits, has not been to avoid speaking like the lower classes ("le bas peuple"). It follows from Brunot's account, that not only all vulgar expressions, but also all tech-

[1] *Bulletin*, 1919, p. 77.

nical terms belonging to handiwork, science, even art, are to be shunned. The language which is to be set up for imitation is the language in use among people who have no profession and only lead the life of high society. This is free from all provincial features, and from all vulgar 'Parisianisms' as well, since people in good society are no more Parisians than they are provincials, they are merely French. All we can say is this, that since they had severally come from some particular place and since they had been in contact with people not belonging to good society, their speech was not always quite pure ("leur usage était trouble"). — Consequently it is the aim of the written language to fix the usage, it is the aim of orthography to direct the pronunciation'.

It would be hard to find a better description of the linguistic movement, which has gone furthest and been pursued most rigorously in France, but which in its main features is to be seen again in many civilized countries. In France the outcome of all these efforts is a highly refined, but at the same time stiff, and in some ways pedantic, language, which has greatly favoured a sort of artistic handling of language and made this to a great extent the common possession of the whole nation, but which on the other hand, with its often narrow and rigorously maintained prescriptions, has been a hindrance to other forms of linguistic art, so that it is no wonder that the Romanticists rebelled against many of the traditional rules laid down by the Academy, though in other fields they were just as subservient to prescription as the most classical writers.

*

(5) After the Aristocratic we take the opposite point of view, the Democratic, which is based on the assumption that in the community one person is just as good as another. The only thing that, according to this point of view, is to be taken into account is the number of those who use a word or a form. In cases of doubt one ought therefore to take a census or have a referendum. But suppose there were 50 per cent on each side, or that three forms had each the same number of adherents? And what should be done with all those people who, if they were honest, would be bound to confess that they did not know what they said, or that they hesitated between two forms? Would it be necessary then to find out statistically the frequency with which they actually used the two forms? It would be obviously impracticable to apply the theory rigidly.

It is strange to see that the point of view described above as the natural-historical, according to which there is nothing right in language, and nothing wrong, is very frequently confused with the 'Majority' theory, as if they were identical. This confusion is found not only in many adherents of the natural-historical point of view, but also in its opponents, for example, Noreen, though the two points of view strictly regarded would seem to be irreconcilable. It is surely one thing to say that everything is equally right or wrong, and another, that everything that the majority does is right.

The Democratic standpoint, here given in its crude form as a mere counting of heads, after which one bows unreservedly to the majesty of the majority and

leaves all minorities to their fate, will hardly find many
to defend it. Yet what is practically the same view,
though in a disguised form, is held by many, perhaps
even by most of those who have theorized on languages. I am referring to the doctrine that Usage is
the highest authority in matters of language. Few
words are so frequently quoted with approval as
those of old Horace:

'si volet usus
Quem penes arbitrium est et jus et norma loquendi'.
'If Usage wills it so, to whom belongs
The rule, the law, the government of tongues'.
(Conington). [1]

One might make a pretty nosegay of sentences of
great philologists, who, more or less clearly, more or
less unreservedly, give their assent to Horace's dictum.
There is Madvig's 'Linguistic usage, once established
and recognized, never errs'; [2] Sayce's, 'The sole standard
of correctness is custom and the common usage of
the community. What is grammatically correct is what
is accepted by the great body of those who speak a
language; [3] Sweet's, 'Whatever is in general use in a
language is for that very reason grammatically correct'. [4]

[1] The translation quoted from Lane Cooper who maintains that
Horace meant by 'usus' only the usage of great writers.

[2] 'Den færdige og anerkendte sprogbrug fejler ikke', 1857,
p. 56. It is however noticeable that this sentence (which of all
Madvig's pronouncements on general linguistic science has been
most frequently quoted in Denmark) is omitted in the German
edition. Did Madvig come to have doubts about it? It would not
be strange, considering that the words 'færdig' and 'anerkendt'
offer easy points of attack to a critic.

[3] *Introd. to the Science of Lang.* II p. 333.

[4] *New Engl. Gram.* § 12.

Even in E. Tegnér's article of 1874, [1] — a quite remarkable one for its time, — from which I quoted
the sentence 'That which, easiliest uttered, is easiliest understood', and in which we find an interpretation of
many linguistic problems far in advance of its time,
we read: 'As a matter of fact a language is nothing
but a fashion prevailing within a certain circle. However absurd the fashion may be, it is still the law of
language, so far as it prevails. There is no higher
authority to appeal to. In so far we may say of it:
Vox populi, vox dei, The voice of the people is the
voice of God!' (p. 109). Again: 'The greatest absurdities in the world become correct, as soon as they
have got Usage fully on their side, just as the worst
usurper becomes legitimate, as soon as he is completely established on his throne. The word 'valfisk'
('whalefish') is an irreproachable Swedish name for
our largest sea-beast, although the beast is not a fish
at all.' (p. 141).

Well, I cannot see that 'valfisk' is one of the worst
things in the world. The name is a quite harmless
outcome of popular zoology — the same analysis of
the animal kingdom which causes lobsters and oysters
to appear in the fish course in a *menu*. [2] The reason
why this word is so frequently adduced as absurd, is
that in this case people may content themselves with the
first part of the word and say a *hval* ('whale'), but
the word in itself is no worse than *marekat* [3] which

---

[1] Reprinted in *Ur språkets värld*, 1922.

[2] We may compare the English *cuttlefish*, *crawfish*, *shellfish*,
ladybird.

[3] Longtailed monkey.

is not a cat, or *marsvin* [1] which is not a swine. The same insect is called in Danish *sommerfugl* and in English *butterfly*, though it is neither a fowl nor a fly. We cannot escape such things because the language was made by practical men and for practical men, and we might equally well complain of the learned specialists, who when they need a scientific name for a sharply marked-off class of a definite description and with quite unmistakeable characters, choose a word for the purpose which previously in popular usage denoted a class which only partially coincides with that for which these learned gentlemen need a name.

But, to deal with the principle involved in Tegnér's statements. The very phrase 'the greatest absurdities' contains a criticism of 'decision by the majority'. If absurdities do harm, (which cannot be said of *hvalfisk)* should we not be justified in fighting against them and trying to get them removed?

Languages, after all, are humanly created, and it is not only a right, but a duty, to contribute to the best of our poor ability to make them better for our fellows and for the generations to come. I am not one of those who recognize the worst usurper as legitimate as soon as he is firmly established on his throne. There is something called political morality which is greater than momentary power. So, as Tegnér's comparison does not produce on me the effect he desired, I dare to declare that there is also a higher linguistic morality than that of recognizing the greatest absurdities when they once have usage on their side. When Tegnér (p. 141) and in like man-

[1] Porpoise: Fr. 'marsouin'.

ner many besides him say that the task of the investigator of language is not to *make* the laws of language, but to describe them, he is right so far as concerns the task of the investigator as such. But at the same time the investigator as a user of the language has the same right as others to influence the language where he can, and he ought to be able by virtue of his greater knowledge to do this with greater insight and greater effect than those who have had no linguistic training.

Noreen is ready to admit that Usage so far gives the pattern of correct speech, that, when other things are equal, (i. e. if the one expression is not better than the other in some other respect), the everyday expression is the best, for the very good reason that it is easier to come at and easier to handle both for the speaker and the person addressed. But he strangely adds that this holds most in regard to pronunciation. Usage, he thinks, has less to do with the forms of words, and least of all with their syntactical employment and meaning. But why in the world not allow Usage exactly the same authority in all domains of language? Here, as at some other points, Noreen's view is wavering and half-hearted.

*

(6) At this point we leave the Democratic standpoint and turn to the Logical standpoint, the standpoint of Thought, which passes judgment on the correctness of an expression according to its agreement with the universal laws of thought. Here then we get something which is established universally, and is

common to all humanity, as opposed both to what is national and what is individual. According to this view, nothing is correct in language which is in conflict with thought. It will be observed that this view goes directly counter to the views of Tegnér and others which have just been discussed, according to which the greatest absurdity becomes right when it has got usage on its side.

Most linguists are against any attempt to apply a logical standard to language. Language, they say, is psychology, not logic; or 'language is neither logical nor illogical, but a-logical'. [1] That is to say, language has nothing to do with logic. To many philologists the very word, logic, is like a red rag to a bull. It cannot be denied that the way in which logic has often been applied in linguistic discussions does not invite imitation, but perhaps that is because it was bad logic, or because it was good logic wrongly applied. It would be surprising however if language which serves to express thoughts should be quite independent of the laws of correct thinking!

In many cases what gives itself out as logic, is not logic at all, but Latin Grammar disguised. Latin has been considered for centuries the supreme language, and extolled for its logic. It was easy then for people to make the mistake of thinking that everything in Latin grammar was pure logic, and that in the other languages only what agreed with Latin could be logically defended The old, in many ways admirable, Danish purist, H. P. Selmer, wrote in 1861 in his book on

[1] So Morf, for example in the Neuphilologentag held at Frankfurt in 1912.

foreign words (I. p. 293): 'An unmistakeable and gross grammatical mistake . . . when we say 'det er mig' ('it is me') . . while according to all laws, human and divine, it ought of course to be 'det er jeg' (it is I') . . it is nothing else than the grossest sin against the first and simplest and most incontrovertible laws of thought and of grammar when in the case under discussion we employ 'mig' . . for 'jeg'.'

There is nothing whatever in logic which obliges the predicative to stand in the same case as the subject, that is, in the nominative. On the contrary the predicative is different from the subject, and in many languages, Russian and Finnish for example, it stands (at any rate very commonly) in other cases such as the instrumental, the partitive, the essive or the translative.[1] Accordingly 'all laws divine and human' and 'the most incontrovertible laws of thought' amount to nothing more than a rule of Latin grammar.

A confusion of a similar kind, by which what is forbidden in Latin grammar is considered as absolutely at variance with the laws of reason, is often found in the condemnation passed by grammarians on constructions in which what in the active is a dative of respect ('the dative object') is turned in the passive into the subject, as in the Greek 'epitetrammai ten phylakēn' 'I have had the guard committed to me', in the English 'he was allowed a sum of money', and in the Danish 'han blev budt hundrede kroner'. There is really nothing in the definition either of the passive or of the different cases to make such combinations absolutely illogical. Whether they are correct or not

[1] See my *Philos. of Gram.* pp. 183, 280.

in a given language must therefore be decided on
other considerations into which I must not enter now.
Let us now examine cases in which logic really has
something to say.

Is it possible that what is purely meaningless, absolutely illogical, may be linguistically correct? Many
linguists answer 'yes'. I will quote the words of two
of the leading men of the old School. Pott writes [1]: 'It
follows that a statement which is perfectly correct as
far as a language is concerned, e. g. 'twice two are
five', need not on that account be true, nay, may sin
grossly against the laws of thought revealed in logic.'
I find similarly in Benfey [2]: 'Anyone, who has once
said 'twice two are five' or 'black is white', knows that
language in and for itself has nothing to do with laws of
thought, but only with its own laws, those of language'.

I have several times put the question to philologists whether the sentence 'mit runde bord er firkantet'
('my round table is square') is correct, and got the
answer that from a linguistic point of view it is irreproachable, while, for example, 'mit rundt bord er
brune', contains two linguistic mistakes. (An English
parallel would be 'mine round table are brown'). They
overlooked the fact that linguistic 'correctness' must attach
just as much to the lexical as to the grammatical element.
The two combinations, 'two and two are five' and 'my
round table is square' are, as sentences, right grammatically, but lexically wrong: because they cannot be harmo-
nized with the meanings of the words 'two' 'five' 'round'.
They are therefore, in reality, linguistically incorrect.

[1] *Intern. Zeitsch. f. allgem. Spr.* I p. 14.
[2] *Geschichte d. Sprachwiss.* p. 10.

It is true enough that the great majority of the speakers who in the course of centuries have fashioned the language have not been acute thinkers, and that languages at many points bear the mark of this defect, even though Lichtenberg goes too far when he insists that 'our whole philosophy is correction of linguistic usage'.[1] But this may still be said in mankind's praise that where expressions which are characterized by the analytical thinker as illogical have taken firm root in a language, closer inspection will show that they are absolutely harmless, because they cannot cause any misunderstanding, and are therefore not at variance with the general function of language. In different languages we frequently find a form used which is attracted into agreement with what immediately precedes it, instead of agreeing with what is more remote, or with the thought as a whole. For example, with indications of plurality. We must admit that the English 'A thousand and one nights' is more logical than the Danish 'tusind og een nat', and that the Danish 'een og tyve dage' is more logical than the Italian *ventun giorno*. In both cases the thought requires the plural, but the speaker is governed by the last word of the combination, *een* and *un(o)*. Meanwhile this usage does not cause the least inconvenience, because the high numeral shows without any doubt that plurality, and not unity, is in question, and we must therefore admit that the indication of plurality in such a case is superfluous, a pleonasm, a luxury.

[1] 'Unsere ganze Philosophie ist Berichtigung des Sprachgebrauches' (quoted from Kretschmer in Gercke and Norden s *Einleit. in die Altertumswiss.* I² p. 465).

We find this confirmed when, apart from these cases of attraction, we see how many languages in certain combinations after a numeral use the singular, because the notion of plurality is made sufficiently clear by the whole combination: *tyve mand høj*, *zwanzig mann*, *twenty stone*. In Magyar indeed and other languages, it is a fixed rule that with a numeral the substantive is in the singular.

In this connexion another rule of language in regard to numerals may be mentioned. We say nowadays in Danish 'een og tyve år', while in earlier days, sometimes at any rate, they wrote 'et og tyve år' The last combination, with the form 'et' agreeing with the neuter word 'år' is perhaps more logical, but the fusion of the compound numeral into a single expression, whereby we avoid the unexpected appearance of an inflexion in the middle of an established combination, is so natural that no one will find fault with it. So we say 'den tre og tyvende' (the three and twentieth), not 'den tredie og tyvende' (the third and twentieth). Compare also group-genitives like 'Kongen av Danmarks magt' 'the king of Denmark's power' No one will find anything illogical here, unless he analyses the expression wrongly, and takes the 's' of the genitive to belong exclusively to the last word 'Denmark', while really, for our linguistic feeling and thought, it belongs to the whole combination 'Kongen av Danmark', 'the king of Denmark'.

In Negations we find a number of phenomena which logicians and grammarians would like to see swept out of the language as sinning against the laws of thought. In many cases, however, the condemnation is based on a superficial logic and a consequent pedantic desire to pose as superior to other people, while a more penetrating analysis and a more intelligent investigation of the psychological origins of the linguistic usage would lead to a more tolerant judgment. In many languages, a doubling, even an accumulation of negatives in the same sentence is very common, or is even required by usage. In these cases it will generally be said that this is wrong because two negatives make an affirmative, just as in mathemathics $- - = +$. I have elsewhere tried to show that the conclusion is incorrect. Language is not mathematics, and two negatives only annul one another when they are attached to the same concept. If that is the case, all languages and all human beings give the two coupled negatives a positive meaning. A double negative with negative meaning only occurs when a number of words not dependent on one another have a negative sign prefixed to them, and in the languages in which this is found those signs are so minute that there is risk of their not being caught if they are only spoken once. The doubling is therefore a sort of assurance against misunderstanding, and cannot be represented as a logical mistake, but, at most, only as a pleonasm.[1]

Where something generally received and employed in the language is condemned as ungrammatical on the ground that it is illogical, as a rule it will appear on closer inspection that the condemnation is the outcome of a narrow view of logic and a narrow view of Grammar, and that a less formally logical consideration of the matter and a freer outlook on the real nature of language, with some understanding of the psychology

[1] *Philosophy of Grammar* p. 331 ff.

of linguistic activity, will join in recognizing that the expression complained of is really justified. The linguistic theorist must therefore set himself against a superficial application of logical standards to questions of correct speech, but in saying this, I say nothing against an intelligent application of logical standards. It is not a proof of logical or grammatical narrowmindedness to set oneself against expressions such as 'he is one of the kindest men that has ever lived', instead of 'that have ever lived'. One can be the enemy of pedantry without surrendering one's liking for clear logic. But we shall have more to say on this when we are treating of 'good language'.

*

(7) Lastly I come to the Artistic Standard, according to which that is correct in language which satisfies our artistic sense, or æsthetic feeling: correct language comes to mean 'beautiful language'. It often happens that when someone is asked whether this or that is correct English (or Danish or French) he will make trial of the two words or expressions either by pronouncing them aloud to himself or considering them in his mind, and then after (so to say) tasting them on his tongue will give it out as his judgment — 'this phrase does not sound well, the other sounds much better' and is therefore correct. When a foreigner asks a native if a certain phrase is correct, he will often get this answer 'Yes, in itself it is all right. I can't give any rule why it should be wrong, but my ear tells me that it sounds bad: it will sound much nicer if you put the words in different order, or use

this word instead of that' etc. But there is no doubt that such an opinion in very many cases rests on a delusion. The man's decision is not really determined by the beauty of the word or the form (which the foreigner might detect for himself) but by his instinctive feeling for what in the foreigner's talk agrees with general usage and is well known to him from earlier linguistic experiences. That is what he is putting to the test when he pronounces the two things to himself. We must clear ourselves of this delusion before we can come in any true sense to an æsthetic appraisement of what is beautiful, but it will be easily seen that this has nothing to do with correctness of speech. On the one hand we have beautiful words lying quite outside what is correct in language (*amare* is a more beautiful word than the English *love* or the Danish *elske*, but is not correct, either as English or Danish). On the other hand in every language we can often choose between two words or phrases, one of which is undoubtedly more beautiful than the other, while both are equally correct. We shall come back to this later. Here we keep strictly to the question of correctness in language unmixed with extraneous considerations.

*

We have now completed our circuit of the seven standards which ordinary people are wont to set up when asked if it is correct to say this or that. It may seem that we are no nearer than we were before. Not one of them has shown that it is capable of being employed as a trustworthy scientific standard which will enable us to pass an infallible judgment in any doubtful cases that may turn up. No external authority can decide everything, and the right of every proposed authority can be questioned. No single district, no single writer or group of writers, no particular upper-class, stands so exalted over all others that its language ought to be followed without reserve. Decision by the majority brings its own doubts and difficulties, and considerations of logic and æsthetics (correct thinking and beautiful speaking) help us only in a small number of cases. Do we arrive then at the purely negative conclusion that the question is insoluble? No, our tour has shown us here and there something that may have a positive significance. It is not entirely reprehensible to desire to have an external authority for the individual to abide by. There is, at any rate in most European countries, a definite non-local form of language, which counts as more elevated than the purely local dialects, and which in many respects, perhaps in most respects, agrees with the language both of the great writers and of the upper-class. But the democratic standpoint has also some justification, and the sound practical sense of the people is shown in this that, rightly regarded, there is not such a great conflict as logicians frequently assert, between the language fixed by the people and that demanded by hard thought. All this however is mere patchwork, and we would fain reach a single standard by which we could pass judgment if this or that, in this language or that language, is correct. I believe we can do so, when we bring the problem into connexion with the whole view of language which has been set forth in the preceding pages. We shall attempt this in the next chapter.

CHAPTER VI

CORRECT AND GOOD LANGUAGE

When we talk of what is right, what is correct, as regards language, these words imply the conception of a 'norm', of something demanded by society, just as in other spheres we have a norm for what is considered right and correct.

We have different ways of behaving ourselves which we employ as custom requires on different occasions, — at a church-service, at a funeral, at social gatherings, when we have to propose a toast, when we meet our superior in the street, etc. All this is demanded by ceremony, and we must behave accordingly if we would be correct. It is just the same with language, except that here the demands made upon us are still more complicated, and in part, at any rate, require to be still more strictly complied with, than the other customs just alluded to.

Our definition of 'that which is linguistically correct' is therefore 'that which is demanded by the particular linguistic community to which one belongs'. What is at variance with this is linguistically incorrect.

If this definition is kept in mind, practically everything is said that need be said. Perhaps however it may be convenient to develop the thought a little further and show how it is marked off from other points of view which have been considered.

*

We may first notice that before anything is recognized as linguistically correct, more is required than that it should be intelligible. If I shift all my tip-of-the-tongue sounds [d, t, n, s] quite forward so that I touch the front teeth, people will say perhaps that I lisp, but all my fellow-countrymen can easily understand me. Still it is not correct Danish (or English) pronunciation. Standard-Norwegian, when pronounced clearly without many specially Norwegian words, is intelligible in Denmark, but is not correct Danish. If I say, 'hvis han har ingenting gjort' or in English 'if he nothing has done' my sentence will be understood. But the correct order of words is in Danish, 'hvis han ingenting har gjort' and in English, 'if he has done nothing' etc. Mere intelligibility is therefore a minimum, and more is required for linguistic correctness. We see this very clearly when we think of foreigners who have been long in the country and acquired great readiness in expressing themselves intelligibly, but who have not attained to that full and exact mastery of the language which will enable us to say of them, that they talk like natives.

We must next insist that the standpoint here given is not the same as that which makes Usage the supreme power over language. First, it is surely an advantage to get, in place of the abstract 'Usage', the more concrete 'Community', i.e. living people, to hold by. And secondly, it is not said that the community's demand upon us is the supreme power from which there is no escape, and that the 'norm' given by the community deserves always to be copied. On the contrary, it follows from what has before been said about the relation between community and individual, that this 'norm' cannot be anything fixed once and for all, because the community consists of particular individuals, and the language of the community (la langue) is only the plural to the way of speaking of the single individual (la parole). The particular person is therefore himself one of the norm-giving class, and may initiate something which in its time, having been adopted by the rest, may become a new norm, in other words, be determinative for the speech of others, so that the correctness of their linguistic usage, of their 'parole', may be judged by it.

There is here a sort of constant tug-of-war between individual and community, an eternal surging backwards and forwards between freedom and linguistic constraint. Full freedom, in the widest sense of the word, there never is, if we wish to communicate our thoughts to others. Even the wildest Dadaists, — who by the way had very little to communicate to their admiring contemporaries, — with all their rebellious wishes about thought and language, could not wholly cut themselves off from the language they were brought up in, but used it, partially at any rate, as their fellow-countrymen did — only worse. From the moment, then, that language is employed on its natural social task, the individual in all essential points is tied to the customs and standing rules of the community, and so can only act freely at his own peril, — 'in freedom and with personal responsibility'.[1] as one who must take the consequences of his acts. On the other hand, the constraint exerted by language is also never complete, because there are only some points in which linguistic usage is absolutely fixed and not to be shaken, and those, as a rule, are points in which the individual feels himself least impelled to assert himself. In countless cases the person who has to use the language has a choice — between a number of nearly synonymous words or between different sentence-constructions, — whereby now this, and now that, is brought to the foreground, and this or that shade of thought comes into view. At any rate, by his intonation or some similar means, he can to a great extent express his personal feeling at the moment.

People often talk of the tyranny of linguistic usage ('usus tyrannus'), and the community is certainly, in the domain of language and in other domains, tyrannical in some of its demands. But this does not imply that the social demand represents what, objectively looked at, is the highest thing possible, or, looked at ethically, the most valuable, what, in the best sense, is the thing most worthy of mankind. In language, as elsewhere, we may often with good reason feel ourselves tempted to rise in rebellion against the 'accursed compact majority'. N. M. Petersen writes:[2] 'What man of high intelligence can find any pleasure in writ-

---

[1] 'I frihed og under ansvar'. (Ibsen).
[2] *Samlede afhandlinger* IV p. 133.

ing[1] a language which he is not allowed to improve? But any intending rebel will soon feel the truth of what the excellent Danish grammarian, Højsgaard, wrote in the middle of the eighteenth century — 'Use and Abuse are sturdy fellows, especially when they grow old!'

Where a fixed spelling is at variance with a fixed pronunciation, one may be permitted to ask if this state of things is worth perpetuating. When I went to school, it was insisted that the old forms of the plurals of verbs must be used in writing: *vi have, elske, ere*, etc., while everybody *said, vi har, elsker, er*, etc. But ought we not to be grateful to those who ventured to break with the old custom in writing, and introduce the new plural forms? It only took a few decads to get these so firmly established that it is now extremely rare to see the old forms. Here, then, good sense has triumphed over a fixed usage in writing, to everybody's advantage, inasmuch as the new forms cause fewer ambiguities than the old, and are an extraordinary relief to all Danes. (In Sweden a similar movement is now beginning.)

We have to do, then, with a centripetal and a centrifugal force — the one tending to discipline, the other to anarchy[2]. Let me quote two utterances of renowned writers which may perhaps throw light on the meaning of social-pressure in language. In his first lectures on *Hovedstrømninger i europæisk litteratur* (I. p. 136 ff.), Georg Brandes made a sharp attack on Society in general, which made an extraordinary sensation at the

---

[1] He might have added, and talking.

[2] Cp. the corresponding conflict in literature, excellently treated by J. L. Lowes, *Convention and Revolt in Poetry* (London 1919).

time, but which, very significantly, he has left out in his *Samlede skrifter* (IV. p. 102). One section of mankind must, according to him, be considered as wild beasts, another as true apes, and the quite overwhelming majority as dunces and ignoramuses. The social formula that they have fashioned has, first of all, the defect that it is general, that is, one thing for all, whereas everything general demands untold sacrifices. (This is the view of society to which Ibsen soon after was to give the classical expression 'Society's God is the spirit of compromise'[1]). But Brandes continues: 'The formula is like a Procrustean bed, on which the Individual is racked and stretched, hewn and polled, until at last he fits the bed. Our language, for example, is something general. We all use the same. It follows that anyone, who wishes to express himself in the language and who possesses some originality, is constrained to make incessant sacrifices. Since he cannot create his expression for himself, but finds it readymade, he is compelled now to say too little, now to exaggerate, now to miss the mark. Not in one case out of a thousand does the language possess a term for the *nuance* of feeling, the quite peculiar sensation, the special impulse, which he wishes to express. All our talking is but an approximation to what we think, inexact, flat and vapid. Hence comes it that so many great writers are inclined to coin words and to use out-of-the-way expressions or comparisons so as to give their language a character of its own. In society this lordship of the general becomes tyranny'. So far, Brandes.

[1] 'Samfundets gud er akkordens ånd' in which Brand sees Satan.

Another side of the question comes out in Schiller's well-known lines:

Weil ein vers dir gelingt in einer gebildeten sprache,
Die für dich dichtet und denkt, glaubst du schon dichter zu sein. [1]

Schiller's saying is directed against one who possesses no more of the soul of a poet than what he has acquired from without himself. But at the same time he gives expression to the weighty thought that the language as a social institution is a mighty help to the individual. From his childhood he has constantly been storing his brain with ready-made forms and expressions of thoughts. These help him to think, and even, to some extent, to find artistic expression for his thoughts.

*

The help which the individual gets from what he receives from the community is naturally the more effective, the firmer fixed the speech-custom is. In Denmark, and no doubt in other countries, there are certain typical formulas which in government offices are eternally used in official communications. So in business language. "We beg to acknowledge the receipt of your esteemed favour", etc.

When one criticizes these expressions, one is often told that it doesn't matter if the formulas are stupid: they have the advantage that people have them ready to hand and need not seek out expressions of their own.

[1] 'Because a verse of thine turns out well in a language of culture which thinks and composes for thee, thou believest at once that thou art a poet'.

It is the same way of thinking which is expressed in the often proclaimed, and for many people, decisive view, that it does'nt matter if a spelling is bad, so long as it is fixed. I notice that Roald Amundsen, when lately interviewed in Norway, being asked 'Why do you use your own orthography?' answered, 'Because we have no orthography'[1]. In this we may perhaps see the same discontent with a want of fixity in spelling, or generally in language, which we meet not unfrequently. But those who cling to fixity as the highest principle, overlook the fact that fixity in spelling leads to a wider and wider cleavage between the spoken and the written language, whereby the latter becomes to each new generation more and more difficult to acquire. By the nature of language changes in speech are unavoidable, and the advantage of an unchanged spelling will scarcely in the long run outweigh the inconvenience caused by the difficulty of acquiring it. The right course here, as elsewhere, is to try to secure a certain flexibility, a power of adapting ourselves to the changes of the times. This is not incompatible with a retention of much of the old system, or at any rate of so much of the old system that there is no breach of continuity.

Even a man, who, on grounds of linguistic history, logic and phonetics, can point to a mass of absurdities in the current spelling, will still persist in keeping in his letters and books a great deal of what he theoretically rejects, just as another, who has the greatest desire to fashion a series of new precise terms for sharply separated concepts, must still, except to an

[1] Reported in *Politiken* 24 July 1924.

infinitesimal extent, use the language in the way he finds it used by his fellow-countrymen. We must pay, and pay dearly, — it is reasonable that we should, — for the great and invaluable advantage of coming into contact with other people, and of being able to impart our thoughts and feelings to them and to share theirs in return. It is therefore no unreasonable demand that the community makes on the individual when. it asks him to surrender something that is his own, and adapt himself in many points to others. But, as men are now constituted, there are a great number who never come to feel this surrender to be a sacrifice. Most of us go on day after day in the same linguistic groove, without having the least inclination in the world except to go on doing exactly like other people. Perhaps it is not such a bad thing that it is so: as Lowell says, 'Human nature has a much greater genius for sameness than for originality, or the world would be at a sad pass shortly'[1].

*

What then is language? An irksome constraint for the highest minds, a supporting staff to the mediocre; or, more truly, to each one of us, now the one, and now the other. The speech-usage of each one of us is constantly swinging backwards and forwards between the demands of society, and an individual expression of his momentary need. We can make this clear by two series of adjectives, though in both series we get some expressions which can be used as terms of praise, and others that can be used as terms of censure. Thus

[1] *Study Windows* p. 56.

on the one hand: the general, level, smooth, everyday, customary, unexceptionable, hackneyed, straightforward, trite, boring, unendurable: they all represent the conventional, what is common to the whole community:

and on the other hand: the uncommon, new, fresh, original, peculiar, personal, eccentric, dare-devil, brilliant: these represent what is individual, proper to a particular person.

*

We have now spoken of two stages of language, *intelligible language*, which made only the minimum claim, and *correct language*, which was more exacting. But we can raise our building still higher — for still greater demands must be made before something is recognized as *good language*. And whilst in the malter of correct speech, if we take it quite strictly, we have only two divisions, a thing being either right or wrong[1], when it comes to the question of *good* language, we have many divisions from the mediocre through the good to the entirely good, and still further, to the remarkable.

And further, we have here two things to take note of: first clearness of thought, what is concerned with the understanding, the purely intellectual side, and then

[1] This does not prevent us of course from setting up as a sort of middle stage what is neither right nor wrong, what is *perhaps* right and *perhaps* wrong. The logical position is the same as that which I postulate in my *Philosophy of Grammar* p. 322 ff. This sphere, in which nothing definite can be said about correctness or incorrectness, is larger than ordinary schoolmasters will admit, the community on account of its own nature and the nature of language being unable to normalize everything.

beauty, or the æsthetic pleasure which can be stirred in the hearer or reader, something that relates to the feelings, something emotional. We propose then the following three stages:

$$\left.\begin{array}{l} \text{intelligible} \\ \text{correct} \\ \text{good} \left\{\begin{array}{l} \text{clear} \\ \text{beautiful} \end{array}\right. \end{array}\right\} \text{language.}$$

Many things may be both intelligible, and correctly expressed, and still neither clear nor beautiful. In the same way a thing may be clear without being beautiful, and *vice versa,* When we touch on clearness and beauty, we are straying into the science of Style, which is properly outside my province. I will say a few words on it, however.

*

When we sit in judgment on goodness of style, can we, and ought we, to pay attention to both sides of Tegnér's formula, 'That which easiliest uttered, is easiliest received'? It seems clear that in the sphere before us, we have only to pay attention to the reci pient. The style is just as good, whether, on the part of the speaker or writer, it is produced with great difficulty and childbirth pains, with many fumbling attempts and corrections, or whether it has sprung to his lips, or to his pen, with a sparkling facility. This applies not only to what is commonly understood by good style, choice of words, combinations of words etc., as they appear in manuscript or in print, but also to what one might call style of utterance, the manner in which the words are produced orally.

Herbert Spencer in a famous essay has treated 'The Philosophy of Style' from the point of view of 'expenditure of energy'. The importance of choice of words, word-position, sentence-building, comparisons etc., lies, he says, in their reducing the strain on the attention of the hearer or reader, in their sparing the mental energy of the recipient. The best style, therefore, is that, by the help of which the purport is seized with least effort. Spencer himself saw that this was perhaps only one side of the 'philosophy of style', (he had not chosen the title himself, but had originally called his treatise, 'Force of Expression'[1]) and there is much truth in the criticism which W. Libby[2] has brought against him, that the important thing is, not so much to economize mental energy, as to stimulate the attention as much as possible ('Not the minimum of effort, but the maximum of response!'). But even this end falls under the 'energetics' of language, and the two points of view are really complementary. At times indeed there may be a conflict between exactness of thought and strength of thought. In such a case everyone must make his choice according to the needs of the moment[3]. There is an inner beauty of language, and an outer beauty. The former, the beauty of sound and 'ring', can certainly be included in the domain of 'energy'. At any rate, the satisfaction or dissatisfaction given us by the sound of words and

[1] See *Autobiog.* I. p. 405.

[2] *Popular Science Monthly*, 1910.

[3] 'Jack London replied to a criticism of his own writings "What the world wants is strength of utterance, not precision of utterance".' (*Times Lit. Supp.* 3 Nov. 1921.)

verbal combinations rests very largely on the ease or difficulty with which the words are produced[1]. Just as the grace of dancing and other movements implies that it is produced with little effort, so, to take only a few examples, we find ugliness in those hardly pronounceable consonant-groups of Oehlenschläger's line:

> Liig brombærrankens grønt gravstenens rune,

or Browning's:

> Spark-like 'mid unearthed slope-side figtree-roots.

The clash of consonants, coupled with the repetition of the sound *as* (or *os*) produces also a very unattractive impression in Giellerup's line:

> Paa svagt glasraslende rimfrosttræer.

The elementary pleasure given us by the rhythmical combinations of words generally employed in poetry is caused by the fact that it is easier for the organs to alternate strong and weak syllables, than to produce long series of syllables all strong or all weak, one after the other. But of course it will be difficult to bring under the category of the 'saving of energy' all the subtler, more musical, effects produced by the harmonious alternation, especially of vowel-sounds, on

---

[1] There is no contradiction, as might perhaps be thought, between what is here advanced and what I said above (p. 133), viz. that our judgment of style is unaffected by the ease or difficulty with which it was first produced. Here we are not concerned with the original author. It is not the beauty of *his* sounds on which judgment is passed, but the beauty of the sounds of the man who reproduces them. The facility with which the latter utters the words is not affected by the fact that the original author may have composed his most euphonious sentences with difficulty.

which so much of the highest pleasure afforded by beautiful verse depends. Here, as in the whole domain of æsthetics, there is something which, at any rate at present, escapes scientific cognition.

This is true to a still greater extent of what we may call the inner beauty of language, which depends on the choice and arrangement of words with regard to all the hidden suggestions of the words and the combinations, and their power to stir the feelings. By such hidden means a writer can at times throw a magic spell over us, of which no analysis, however penetrating, can enable us to find the reason or the laws of its working. But we have now got far away from — and far above — the question of correct speech as determined by the community, which was the starting point of our train of reflexion.

*

We may now leave the consideration, both of linguistic correctness, which we defined as what was demanded by the community, and of good language. In dealing with the former we made no use of either part of Tegnér's formula, 'that which easiliest uttered, is easiliest received', with the latter we made use only of the second half — regard to the recipient. But we have still not done with the valuation of language: there remains a kind which we have hinted at already here and there. This is marked off from the two kinds so far spoken of by not being concerned, as they are, with the individual and his utterance (his 'parole'), but with the community as a whole and its 'language'. For this can also be appraised, by measuring its value (or the value of some item of it), in relation to a linguistic ideal. When we thus pass our judgment, we shall be compelled, as we were not compelled in the previous cases, to pay respect both to the producer or producers and to the recipients and readers of the language, because the ideal human language must be that which by the simplest and easiest possible means is able to express human thoughts in the fullest manner and in the manner which is easiest for the recipient.

We can inquire into the value of details in a language. We do so, in fact, very often, when we complain of the ambiguities caused by the German use of *Sie*, or the Danish use of *De*, as the pronoun for the second person singular, or of the English *you* being used in addressing one person or several, or of the misunderstanding occasioned by such sentences as 'j'ai fait faire un habit à Jean', or 'die frau, die meine schwester bewundert' etc.. or of the inconveniences of two words being sounded alike, shown in Henry Bradley's story of the man who was singing the praises of .Oxford, and burst out with 'And what a whole (= hole!) it is!'

These examples may serve to show the essential difference between the inquiry we have now entered on, and our previous inquiry as to how far a form or an expression was linguistically correct. The Danish 'De kommer' and the German 'Sie kommen' are correct sentences, whether they mean 'they come' or 'you come'. Similarly the sentences quoted from French, German and English are unimpeachably correct, but it would have been better if these languages had been so contrived that such ambiguities should have been impossible. This may be admitted, whether the inconveniences are considered great or trifling. But it is important to insist that a thing may be linguistically correct, and yet far from ideal, if looked at objectively. We see the same thing indeed, whenever we notice that a language has no expression for some thought which other languages can express. Most languages are without any word equivalent to *gentleman*. English has no word for Germ. *fach*, Dan. *fag*. Danish has the word *fordel*, 'advantage', but no corresponding word for 'disadvantage'. The usual way of getting over a recognized deficiency of this sort is by simply introducing a foreign word. But whoever does this, or seeks to fill the void by creating a new word within the framework of his own language, even the man of science who introduces a new expression for some concept recognized by himself but hitherto not expressed in the language, ought constantly to take both parts of Tegnér's formula into account, and ask himself if the word or expression is easy to handle both to the speaker and to the hearer. Unless he does so, he is not paying proper regard to those whom he wishes to use his new words in the future.

*

Then we have the criticism of a language as a whole This often takes the form of a comparison between a particular language and other languages, and we hear it said that Italian is one of the most musical languages, that French is distinguished by logical clarity, or Greek by variety and plastic beauty, or English by its richness and manly strength, or whatever other character people may assign to it. More valuable scientifically than generalities of this kind is a comparative valuation of a language with the same language at an earlier stage, in order to throw light on the question, if the language has progressed or receded in historical times, or, on the more general question that arises from it, if the changes that take place in languages can be described on the whole as progress, or as decline or degeneracy. This is the question I propounded in Chapters XVII and XVIII of my book *Language*. I there tried to point out that language on the whole had progressed, and that, from the point of view both of the speaker and of the hearer, it might be considered as better now than in the earlier stages of its evolution.

*

It is only by regarding things in this light that we can understand the apparent paradox that linguistic evolution takes place through constant 'mistakes' or sins against what has been hitherto counted as correct usage, and yet may lead to beneficial results. It has often been observed by students of language that (to give only a single quotation) "The history of language, when looked at from the purely grammatical point of view, is little other than the history of corruptions" (Lounsbury). It was precisely this fact, that what was considered a bad mistake in one century, is recognized in the next century as absolutely correct, that, as already mentioned, was the most important reason why linguistic historians were so disinclined to concern themselves with questions of 'right' or 'wrong' in language, and managed even to come to the conclusion

that from a scientific point of view there was nothing
in language which could be called correct or incorrect.
But we can rise above this purely negative standpoint,
and get a really rational method of appraising language,
when we understand:

(1) what the linguistic community properly is, and what
its relation is to the individuals who compose it;

(2) that correct speech means the speech which the
community expects, and mistakes in speech mean
departures from that — quite without regard to the
inner value of the words or forms;

and (3) that there is — entirely independent of this, —
a valuation of language in which its value is meas-
ured by reference to a linguistic ideal, which perhaps cannot be entirely contained in Tegnér's phrase,
but of which one of the most important elements is
the energetic formula 'that which easiliest uttered, is
easiliest received'

*

It is clear that this last way of regarding languages
is of special importance when it is attempted to con-
struct an artificial language for use in international intercourse. Here the problem is to get a language of-
fering as little friction as possible. This is expressed
in a formula which I first put forth in the preface to
Couturat and Beaufront's Ido-French Dictionary, 1908,
and which has since played a great rôle in the linguistic deliberations of Idists: — 'that language is the best
which at every single point is easiest to the greatest
possible number of human beings'

CHAPTER VII

THE STRATIFICATION OF LANGUAGE

We have often already (in the chapters on Standard Language and on Linguistic Correctness) had occasion to remark that the social stratification of a country leaves its mark on the language of individuals. We speak of an 'upper class' language and a 'lower-class' language: 'the classes and the masses' are distinguished by their speech as much as by their clothes and way of thinking. In every modern novel one may see, for example, the difference between the language of a judge and that of an ordinary workman. Similarly in the old Indian drama of many centuries ago there were two distinct forms of language, sanskrit *(samskrta,* elegant language), spoken by gods, kings, princes, brahmins etc., down to dancing-masters, and prakrit *(prakrta,* natural or simple language) spoken by men in inferior positions, such as shopkeepers, officers of justice, policemen, bath-masters, fishermen, and by nearly all women. It would of course be absurd to make out two such sharply-marked classes in modern life, one above and one below. The social, and with it also the linguistic stratification, is extremely varied, and there are all sorts of links between the highest and the lowest. Every single person throughout his life is constantly hearing the talk of people drawn from a number of social strata, and is himself more or less affected by their ways of speech.

His own speech is not the same at all times. His tone in conversation and, with it, his choice of words change with the stratum of society in which he finds himself at the moment. It goes with this that the language takes a different colour from the mere subject of the conversation: we have one style for a love-declaration, another for an official pronouncement, another for a rough rebuff or reprimand, etc. About stylistic strata of this sort, I shall say nothing. I must dwell a little, however, on the fact that a given person comes naturally to talk in a different way according to the person he is with at the moment. As Chaucer somewhere says, in talking to ordinary people one does not use the same "Heigh style, as whan that men to kinges wryte." The stratification depends then not only on the position of the speaker, but on that of the person addressed.

There is not however much to be said about this distinction so far as European countries nowadays are concerned. In regard to grammar it shows itself most in the fact that in many languages a special pronoun is used for the second person when one is addressing a superior, or a stranger to whom one wishes to be polite For this purpose plural forms are often employed. This goes back to the habit of the Roman Emperors (and of kings even now) of speaking of themselves as *we* and requiring to be addressed as *Ye*, as though they were several persons in one. The address with 'ye' was in later times extended, and hence the French *vous*, the Russian *vy*, as opposed to the familiar French *tu*, *toi*, Russian *ty*. In English, at one period, a distinction (still persisting in some rustic dialects) was made between the familiar *thou* and the more formal *you (ye)*. But the polite form was afterwards applied more and more widely, till in ordinary English everyone, as at present, was addressed as *you*. In German, *Ihr*, as the form of address to a single person, has been driven out by *Sie*, originally a pronoun, not of the second person at all, but of the third, and this is imitated by Danes and Norwegians in their use of *De*. In Dutch the old word for 'thou' has passed entirely out of use, so that *gij*, which corresponds to *ye*, is used in familiar address (where the French would use *tu*), and a new expression for polite address, *U* (originally *Uwe edelheid*), has been introduced. In Italian, there are three stages of increasingly respectful address, *tu*, *voi*, *lei*. In Spanish the pronoun of polite address is *Usted*, an abbreviation of *vuestra merced* ('Your Grace'.)

Here we see how at times mere pronouns are not sufficient, and people are compelled, or from social considerations fancy themselves to be compelled, to use titles. So in some countries a lady is not addressed as 'you', but is spoken of to her face as 'Frau —', 'Fru —', ('Mrs. —',) — the same with a Professor, Councillor, Prince (in Danish, 'Deres excellence', 'Deres kongelige højhed', 'Deres majestæt' etc.). This is a serious inconvenience in Denmark, Norway and Germany, but worse in Sweden, where a mistaken and exaggerated courtesy constantly prevents the use of the pronoun of address, *ni*.

In this connexion we see that reaction against the disposition to make class-distinctions has caused the English and American Quakers (the Society of Friends) to frame, what one might call, a religious or sectarian dialect (though only in a small area of the grammar of the language). In the seventeenth century, when the Quakers came into being, it was customary in English, as has been said, to make the distinction between *thou* as the familiar, and *you* as the more submissive pronoun of address. As the Quakers with their strong religious feeling of equality would not have anything to do with this distinction, but wished to address everyone in the same way as in the time of Christ, they decided in all cases to use the Biblical *thou*. As a matter of fact, ordinary Quakers however did not understand the Biblical distinction between the two cases *thou* and *thee*, nor rightly grasp the verbal-endings required by that pronoun. The result was that, where ordinary Englishmen said *you give*, they said *thee gives*. They even used this form in the plural, introducing into their dialect the feature of ordinary English that the pronoun of the second person was the same in the two numbers. Thus *thee gives* came to represent both *thou givest* and *ye give* as used in the language of the Bible.

*

What we Europeans however suffer in regard to language from social inequality is nothing compared to what we find with Orientals, whose language reflects an absolutely cringing subservience. The Japanese have different words, not only for *thou* or *you*, but for *I*, according to the person addressed. How far they have gone in this direction may be seen. from the fact that the most familiar words for 'I' and 'thou', *boku* and *kimi*, used by children in addressing their friends and playfellows, but not otherwise used at all, originally meant 'servant' and 'lord'. In Basque there are not only different pronouns, but different verbal-forms, so that 'I have' must be differently put according as one is talking to one's subordinate, one's equal, or one's superior. The Burmans, when they are addressing a superior, introduce a special particle *taunin* or something similar, into the verb; e. g. *pru-thi*, (I make) becomes in this situation, *pru-taumu-thi*. The natives of Java, besides their common language *ngoko*, have a special dialect for addressing people of princely rank, called *krama*. Between these two, there is *madya*, a sort of cut-down *krama*. Further, there is *basa kadaton*, the 'language of the palace', and finally, *krama inggil*, used by subordinates when talking together about persons of rank. This last may only be used by princes when they are talking about themselves. The special words in *krama* are partly words taken from other languages such as Malay, Sunda or Sanskrit, partly words of the ordinary language altered by means of new prefixes or suffixes or changes of sound. Or they may be circumlocutions. [1]

Another dialect used with regard to the person ad-dressed is that more or less affected nursery-language

[1] Fabre, quoted by Niceforo GA p. 252.

which many mothers and nurses are much inclined to use with small children — where 'stomach' is 'tumtum', 'horse' is 'gee-gee', 'thank-you' is 'ta' etc. It is generally used in the quite mistaken belief that the little ones understand this language more easily than ordinary English. As a matter of fact, the use of this affected language makes things more difficult for the children. They will have to learn correct English some time and will learn it all the more easily and more rapidly if they never hear anything that is not perfectly correct. In many countries people talking to children use a number of diminutives, and not unfrequently in various languages give a caressing tone to a number of consonants by palatalizing them (making them mouillés).

Here I must also mention some very remarkable things which Sapir has noticed in the language of the Nootka Indians of Vancouver Island.[1] Here certain physical characteristics of the person addressed or spoken of are indicated by the form of language employed, great resort being made to consonantal play In speaking to a child or about a child, it is usual to add the ordinary diminutive suffix. This serves merely to imply a friendly feeling. So -'is is inserted before terminations which indicate tense, mood or person in the verb. In addressing or speaking of persons of unusual size, *aq* is inserted similarly. In addressing or speaking of dwarfs or very little people, the diminutive suffix is used as before, and in addition all sibilants are palatalized. These forms with palatalized *s'* are also used when one is talking about

[1] *Abnormal Types of Speech in Nootka*, Ottawa, 1915.

little birds, such as sparrows and wrens. The diminutive suffix is also used to and of people who have lost an eye, or who squint, or have some other such defect, but in their cases all s or ſ sounds are changed into the corresponding unvoiced side-sounds (different variants of *l*). It is noticed however that the people so addressed are inclined to be offended when these forms are used: so that the forms are only used derisively or by way of teasing. Humpbacked people are also spoken of with use of the diminutive suffix, but the ordinary s and ſ sounds are now changed to some peculiar 'thickish' ſ sounds, pronounced with the lower jaw somewhat protruded, the diminutive *is* becoming *ic*, where *c* denotes this peculiar variety. of sound. In talking of lame people, an element L [voiceless lateral affricative] or Lſ, is inserted somewhere or other in the word, and with left-handed people the element tſH is inserted after the first syllable of the word. The same form is used in speaking of bears, who are considered in popular belief to be left-footed. In speaking of greedy people, tſx is inserted after the first syllable and this is also done in speaking of the raven, which in the popular superstition is described as specially voracious. There is no particular inserted-sound used in connexion with cowards, but they may be made ridiculous, when spoken of or addressed, by making the voice small, i. e. speaking with a thin piping voice to denote cowardice.

Many of the above mentioned linguistic changes are used, not only in scorn, but sometimes in a more goodnatured way when the person in question is present. The speaker then wishes kindly to suggest that he does not attach any great importance to the particular defect.

It is also worth noting that in the folk-sagas and songs of the Indians some animals are characterized by the changed form of the words put in their mouths. So in the story of the hart and the mink (the mink is a sort of marten or polecat), the Nootka change all sibilants into l-like sounds, while the Kwakiutl characterize the animals by the contrary transposition, and so with other transpositions of consonants. Sapir mentions that the Indians are not the only people to use sound-play of this sort. He has found parallels among the Bushmen. Meinhof [1] also asserts that in African animal-stories, every animal has its special language.

[1] *Die moderne Sprachforsch. in Afrika* p. 122.

CHAPTER VIII

SLANG

What was said in earlier chapters about the freedom, or want-of-freedom, of the individual in relation to what is conventional in language, naturally brings us to treat of Slang, a form of speech which actually owes its origin to a desire to break away from the commonplaces of the language imposed on us by the community. But it is important to keep this side of the matter in view and to separate slang as sharply as possible from other kinds of language with which it is often confused. The ordinary Slang-Dictionaries include, not only what is slang in the proper sense, but words from thieves-language (which will be treated in Chapter X), and vulgarisms, (which have their proper place in the discussion of the social stratification). It is also of course quite reprehensible when these motley collections are given a *local* designation, as though the most significant thing about the words was that they were used in some particular Capital. I am thinking of such titles as Villatte's *Parisismen* and Baumann's *Londonismen*, or Sainéan's *Le langage parisien.* One form of language may indeed shade into another: — but here we shall make an attempt to bring out the fundamental differences.

The ultimate impulse to the creation of Slang is a certain feeling of intellectual superiority. We find that some particular word or expression of the normal language has grown trite, it is too well known, we are sick of it, and so we seek for a new word, that will tickle the fancy and satisfy our desire for something amusing, or at least pleasurable, by way of a change. Slang is an outcome of mankind's love of play ('spiel-trieb'): it is the playful production of something new, where, properly speaking, nothing new was required. In the light of pure reason, the old word is good enough: it is only our feelings that cannot stand it any longer. Slang is a linguistic luxury, it is a sport, and, like any other sport, something that belongs essentially to the young. It is (or was, at any rate) a greater favourite with young men than with young women. One may briefly describe it as the fight against what is outworn and drab. At times it takes a somewhat dare-devil character: but at other times it must be described as really poetical: in many of the transferred uses of words found in Slang, there is a really poetic fancy which may be highly refreshing.

A slang-expression by its very nature must be fresh: but it follows from this very fact that when it has been in use for a certain time, it no longer has the effect implied in its name. A slang-word which has been used too frequently is as depressing as a story we have often read before, or an old joke. Slang, then, must be often renewed. Many slang-words, however widely they are known for a short time, have but a very brief existence.

Slang springs up in some particular place, and there in an astonishingly short time it may win wide acceptance. Some words have the good fortune to spread over the whole nation, whilst others are only used locally. Each of the two sister-universities, Oxford and Cambridge, has a number of Slang-words which are unknown to the other. It is the same with Philadelphia and New York, though they are only a two hours' railway-journey apart.

When once in New York I asked for an explanation of a number of Slang-words in a new book *Fables in Slang* by the Chicago author, George Ade, my friends there in many cases had to confess their ignorance.

On the other hand, many words, which sprang up originally as Slang, fixed themselves so fast in course of time, that no one remembers now that they were originally meant as a refreshing luxury. They have become part of the ordinary stock of the language. These are the things that make the study of Slang so attractive, while they make it difficult sometimes to draw the line between Slang and other branches of language.

*

In many schools, especially in old boarding-schools in which the boys live together on very intimate terms, often quite cut off from other people, and often with the feeling that they are a specially privileged class, a particular language is evolved of which the essential constituent is Slang. Dictionaries of such school-dialects have been made, e. g. for Winchester College and for Herlufsholm School in Denmark.[1]

A characteristic feature of the last dialect is that the words are formed by taking the beginning of the word and joining the end on to it, omitting the middle-sounds. For example *tælk* stands for *tykmælk* and *tonen* for *tykmælkkonen*. But along with this there are many distortions of words which appear to be quite arbitrary, and new words arbitrarily formed just as in Winchester language, and in the special dialect which has developed on such a large scale in the military school, the Ecole Polytechnique, in France.[2] One may sometimes be in doubt whether these school-languages should not be classed under languages of concealment, languages . constructed to be understood merely by the initiated, rather than under playful-language, slang-language in the proper sense of the word.

Again, the common-life led by soldiers, in peace, and still more in war, gives birth to a number of Slang-formations, such as have frequently been studied, especially in connexion with the World-War of 1914—18. [3]

*

[1] R. G. K. Wrench, *Winchester Word-Book*, Winchester and London, 1891; Ebbe Neergård, *Ordbog over skolesproget på Her-lufsholm* (Privately printed. København 1922): J. Marson, *Skorpe-sproget, (Danske Studier* 1922 p. 67 ff.) Cp. also R. Eilenberger, *Pennälersprache* (Strassburg, 1910): J. Meier, *Hallische Studenten-sprache* (Halle, 1894): F. Kluge, *Deutsche Studentensprache* (Strass-burg, 1895).

[2] See *Mémoires de la Soc. de Linguistique XV.*

[3] In this branch of literature I need only mention Karl Larsen, *Dansk soldatersprog til lands og til vands* (Kjøbenhavn, 1895).

Slang is jesting-language. There is always a humorous element in Slang: the new words are meant to be a pleasant change from the old. Philologists have not always noticed this. Thus Sainéan,[1] after treating of the transformation of words by giving them arbitrary endings, so frequent in French slang, and the greater and greater complications which ensue, as when *filou* is turned into *philanthrope*, *philibert* or *philosophe* (the last is used of a card-cheat), goes on: ' It would be a waste of time to look for allusions of a humorous or any other kind in these slang perversions. They are ruled by chance and guided by caprice.'

It is quite true that transformations of this kind are not the highest kind of humour, and that a learned philologist may at times find them flat and pointless. But those who invent such transformations, or employ them, do without any doubt get vast amusement out of them, at any rate for a time. This was evidently the case with the first inventor of the form *brolly* for *umbrella*. People who in Danish say *frikadonse* for *frikadelle* and *melodonte* for *melodi* also imagine that these transformations of everyday words are funny. On the other hand people of more refined taste will

P. Schjærff. *Den danske Jens og hans sprog.* *(Danske studier* 1918 p. 119 ff.) O. Mausser. *Deutsche soldatensprache* (Strassburg, 1917). L. Sainéan, *L'argot des tranchées*, (Paris, 1915). A. Dauzat, *L'argot de la guerre* (Paris, 1918). G. Esnault, *Le poilu tel qu'il se parle* (Paris, 1919). C. Alphonso Smith, *New Words self-defined* (New York, 1920). E. Fraser and J. Gibbons, *Soldier and Sailor Words and Phrases* (London, 1925).

[1] *L'argot ancien* p. 59.

avoid them and be content to use the words in their normal forms.

Amusing examples of a slang of her own used by Mrs. S. T. Coleridge are given by Robert Southey in a letter of 14th sept. 1821. Here are some of them:

"when she is red-raggifying in full confabulumpatus. True it is that she has called us persecutorums and great improprietors for performing this meritorious task, and has often told us not to be such a stuposity; threatening us sometimes that she will never say anything that ends in lumpatus again; and sometimes that she will play the very dunder; and sometimes bidding us get away with our toadymidjerings. And she asks me how I can be such a Tomnoddycum, and calls me detesty, a maffrum, a goffrum, a chatterpye, a sillycum, and a great mawkinfort . . You are not a vulgarum, nor a great ovverum govverum . . you are a stumparumper, because you are a shortycum; and you are a wattlykin, a tendrum, a detestabumpus, and a figurumpus . . . If my foot happens to touch her chair, I am told that anything whidgetting the chair makes her miseroboble. If the children — the childeroapusses I should say — are bangrampating about the house, they are said to be rudderish and roughcumtatherick. Cuthbert's mouth is called sometimes a jabberumpeter, sometimes a towsalowset' etc. Most of the ways of forming and transforming words which occur in ordinary Slang and in nursery-language are here united as in a sample-collection.

*

It has been said that Slang is a fresh, boyish language, employed chiefly as an escape from hackneyed words. It is therefore natural that in the Slang of all countries there are certain common-features appearing again and again. Behind what is individual and national we find here, as everywhere, what belongs to our common humanity. If we only give a little rub to the special case, we shall quickly elicit a spark of the human nature, common to us all.

Some things, more than others, seem everywhere to provoke the use of Slang. And, if anyone will undertake a comparative study of the Slang of different countries, — for this purpose he can make large use of the lists of synonyms given in Farmer and Henley's great seven-volume Dictionary [1] — he will find that, with inevitable variations, the same or similar pictures and metaphorical uses of words are everywhere repeated.

Among the favorite objects of Slang, one may mention first and foremost the different parts of the body. So

The head (and brain, especially as the seat of the understanding). Here we first meet with comparisons with different fruits: Danish *pære*, Engl. *nut*, *cocoanut* (this is so general that in the corrupt English of the Polynesians, Beach-la-mar, it has become the ordinary word for 'head'), *onion*, *turnip*, *pumpkin*, *calabash*, *costard;* French, *poire*, *noisette*, *coco*, *citron*, *citrouille;* German, *kürbis*.

Then we have words which more or less correspond to the Danish *krukke* (a crock, pitcher); it is an interesting thing here that the ordinary French

[1] *Dictionary of Slang and its Analogues*, (London 1905).

word for the head, *tête*, was originally a slang-word, the Latin *testa*, meaning a pitcher or potsherd, and that the Germ. *Kopf* has in like manner lost its slang-character, though the same word as *cup*. Both in French and German the old and more respectable names for 'head' have been kept, but are now used in a colourless, more metaphysical sense — French *chef* from Latin *caput*, and Germ. *haupt*. To this class of Slang-words belong the Eng. *chump* (properly, lump), *crust*, no doubt also *top-knot;* French *boule*, *bille*, *balle*, (notice the assonance in these three), *caisson*.

Lastly we have Slang-words for 'head', denoting it as the highest part of the body, the body itself being compared with a house. Hence the Danish *øverste etasje* (especially in the phrase, 'han er ikke rigtig i øverste etasje', 'he is not right in the top storey', English *upper storey*, [1] *attic*, *garret*, *cockloft*, *upper loft*, *upper works;* Germ. *oberstübchen*, *oberer stock;* Fr. *ardoise*, *grenier à sel;* Span. *chimenea* (chimney).

Other comparisons are seen in Fr. *bobine* (bobbin), *fiole* (little bottle).

The Nose. Danish, *snude*, (snout), *snydeskaft* &c.; Engl., a number of expressions: *beak*, *peak*, *snout*, *proboscis* (learned!), *smeller*, *snuffbox*, *snorter*, *snorer*, *posthorn*, *nozzle*, *handle*, *trumpet*, *snottle-box*, *candlestick*, *bowsprit;* in pugilistic language we find

---

[1] 'He is gone in the upper storey' = Fr. 'il a une araignée dans le plafond ('he has a bee in his bonnet') = Du. 'hij mankeert het (het scheelt hem) in zijn bovenkamer,' (he has something wanting in his upper chamber).

the delightful *claret-jug, claret* being used of blood; French, *trompe, trompette, piton.*

The Hand. Eng. *paw.* Dan. *pote,* Germ. *pfote.*

The Leg — the Feet. Eng., *creepers, trotters,* (nursery language), *trampers, drumsticks, trespassers, pegs;* Dan. *undersåtterne* (underlings); French, *trottins, brancards, flûtes (jouer des flûtes,* take to his heels), *le train onze (prendre le train onze* = aller à pied).

It would be too prolix to go through similar lists of Slang-expressions for different parts of the body. I can merely indicate other areas in which slang-words spring up with special luxuriance. Words meaning to cudgel, scold, chatter, steal, run, foods and drinks, the condition one finds oneself in after too much alcohol; further, words for money, all imaginable terms of abuse, mostly perhaps of stupid people and stupidity, the clever liking to show their superiority to the dull by finding out all possible contemptuous expressions for dolts. Contempt, particularly, is one of the emotions which most frequently find an outlet in Slang, side by side with the purely innocent delight in finding humorously-exaggerated expressions. Contempt often shows itself in ironical phrases in which an expression comes to mean exactly the opposite of its proper meaning, as when 'a nice fellow' comes to mean 'a frightful scoundrel', or 'much he knows about it' to mean that he knows very little indeed.

Irony is often seen in nicknames. I take a few examples from literature which have certainly been caught up from real life. 'Dead Andrew, so called because his father had been taken for dead but had come to life again'[1] (Goldschmidt, *Sam. Skr.* VIII p. 320). 'A little fisherman, called 'The beauty' because of his great ugliness'[2] (Andersen Nexø, *Muldskud* p. 60). — Even among the Indians this is found: a tribe was called by its neighbours Katáiimiks, 'Notlaughers', 'because they were always laughing' (Uhlenbech, *Geschlachts- en persoonsnamen der Peigans* p. 9).

Not unfrequently an association of ideas is carried further in Slang than in the sober normal-language. Let me take a few examples from English. It is natural to say 'Keep your head' in the sense, 'Keep your presence of mind', or again to say, 'He lost his head'. But this is extended to such a point that people say 'Keep your hair on', and (as *wool* is Slang for 'hair'), 'Keep your wool on'. *To go the whole hog* is used for 'to carry a course of conduct to extremities'. This is then improved on, and we get *go the whole animal, go the entire animal, go the extreme animal,* (this last in Dickens). The expression, *my better half* for 'my husband' or 'my wife', I have found improved into my better seven-eighths'. There is a political expression which has recently spread from America to England, which has its basis in a similar extension. It is quite natural to say of a political candidate, 'he stands on the Repub-

---

[1] 'Døde Anders hed sådan, fordi hans fader havde været skindød, men var kommen til live.'

[2] 'En lille fisker, 'Dobbeltskøn' kaldet som følge av sin store grimhed.'

lican platform'. 'Platform' then comes to mean the
party-programme as a whole ('Lincoln was elected
on a platform which declared that the Constitution
was to be disregarded.'). From this we get the use
of 'a plank' for a single item in the party-programme.

The well-known German philologist, Karl Müllenhoff,
in his schooldays and later was called Cato because
his father was a Catholic (he was not one himself).
When his younger brother went to the school, h e was
called Lælius. (*Cato* and *Lælius* were two treatises
of Cicero generally read in the school.) [1]

Another method by which Slang gets a number of
its expressions is by shortening the normal-word. This
may serve to throw light on the difference between
Slang and the secret language of thieves, which I shall
treat later under the name 'concealment-language'. In
his book above-mentioned Sainéan distinguishes between *l'argot ancien* and *l'argot moderne*, and says
that the shortening of words which is so frequent
in the latter is not known in the former. That is just
because the so-called old 'argot' is thieves-language,
in which such a curtailing of words would not be
practical, since the chief object of the 'argot' was to
render words unrecognizable. This method of proceed-
ing is therefore unsuitable in a 'concealment-language'
while it is affected in Slang, where it plays an im-
mense rôle, chiefly perhaps in school and university
Slang. Here for instance in English we have *lab* for
laboratory (French *labo*), *gym* for *gymnasium*, *maths*
for *mathematics*, French *desse* for (*géométrie*) *de-
scriptive* &c. Other French curtailings are *pneu* for

[1] Scherer, *Müllenhoff* 1896, p. 15.

pneumatique, *vélo* for *vélocipède*, *le métro* for (*chemin de fer*) *métropolitain*, *perme* for *permission* (military). Many such curtailed forms have passed from Slang into the ordinary language, e.g. *kilo* (over all Europe) for *kilogram*, *piano* for *pianoforte* (*or fortepiano;* the original name was the clumsy Italian, *grave cembalo col piano e forte*, which it is not surprizing that people could not put up with for long), *auto* (French, German &c.) and in Scandinavia *bil* for *automobil*, English *cab* for *cabriolet*, *bus* (also in other languages) for *omnibus*, English and French *photo* for *photograph(ie)*. The character of these curtailed words is so well known and has been so often discussed that I need not give more examples. I will mention however some French slang-curtailments not generally known: *cé mess (maisse)* for *ces messieurs* as a playful name for the police: it is treated as a collective substantive with the feminine article, *la cémaisse* like *la police*. *Def* was used by Apaches (Hooligans) to mean a hat or cap. This is short for *Desfoux*, the name of a hatter in the Rue de la Monnaie, from whom they bought the articles about 1880.[1]

It is worth notice that the inclination to make frequent use of these curtailed forms of words is especially strong in the overcivilized society of our times with its accelerated *tempo* as contrasted with the timeless life, of orientals for example, in which there is nothing that can be called hurry, and in which a sentiment like 'time is money' is unthinkable. (For most of us time is more than money!) And further it is noticeable that this curtailment specially attacks

[1] Niceforo GA. p. 230, Sainéan LP. p. 265.

long foreign words, whose single components convey nothing to the mind. The abbreviations by the use of initial letters which have been spreading of late years (e. g. Y. M. C. A.) — both that kind in which the single letters are read, and that in which these letters are formed into a word (e. g. Dora = Defence of (the) Realm Act) — are also a new thing in our own day. They presuppose considerable proficiency in reading.

With these curtailed forms we also get a humorous extension of linked-thoughts, when schoolboys in England shorten the word *dictionary* to *dic*, — but then, *Dick* being a petname for *Richard* — call the dictionary *Richard*. In the same way contrariwise a *william* is used for a 'bill' in the sense of an account for payment or (U. S. A.) a banknote.

*

In many cases a word is at the same time curtailed and extended, or, to put it differently, the beginning of a word is taken, and completed by means of some meaningless termination, as in the Danish *frikadonse* for *frikadelle*. In French there are many stumpwords which naturally end in - o, as the above-named *auto*, *photo*, *métro*, and *typo* for *typographe,* (in these words the *o* is the final stem-sound of an element in a Greek compound): further *vélo*. But this ending in *o* is transferred to other curtailings in which the original word does not contain this vowel: *Montparno* for *Montparnasse*, *apéro* for *apéritif*, *camaro* for *camarade*, *pharmaco* for *pharmacien*. In English the termination *o* is used in exclamations, *righto! cheerio!*

— even, as here, after complete words. We have this
termination with a curtailed word in *beano* for *bean-
feast*. A termination *-er* is general with curtailed
words; e. g. *footer* for *football*, *fresher* for *freshman*,
brekker (Harrow) for *breakfast*, *bonner* for *bonfire*,
heeler for *heeltap*, *bedder* for *bedmaker* (Cambridge)
or *bedroom* (Oxford), Again *-y* (*-ie*) is very commonly used, partly because it recalls the adjective-
ending, e. g. in *cumfy* for *comfortable*, *luny* for *lu-
natic*, partly as a substantival diminutive-ending (in
baby, auntie) e. g. in *Algy, Algie* for *Algernon*, *Tuppy*
for *Tupman*, *nighty* for *night-dress*, *bookie* for *book-
maker*. But further there is an interesting class of
words with an inserted *g*: *Wuggins* at Oxford for
Worcester College, *wagger pagger bagger* for *waste
paper basket* and many more, (besides those given in
Language p. 300).

One may remember at this point that in the twen-
ties of the last century, after a diorama had had a
great success in Paris, it became the fashion in Slang
to add the termination *-rama* or *-orama* to all possible words: so in Balzac's *Père Goriot* we have
santérama, *froitorama*, *soupeurama*. Another sort
of addition made to a word is the so-called *queue
romantique*, by which *crème*, for example, as applied
to a man who is made a fool of by his accomplices,
is extended to *creme au chocolat*, which may then
be cut down to the one word *chocolat*.[1]

A particular form of Slang-extension consists in
adding one or more meaningless words, riming with
the last word in a sentence which has just been ut-

[1] Esnault, *Le poilu*, p. 153.

tered. I remember one example from the days of my childhood:

Det veed vi, det veed vi
min datter Hedvig.[1]

In French, there is a great liking for such additions to set phrases: ça colle, Anatole! | Tu parles, Charles! | Un peu, mon neveu! | comme de juste, Auguste![2] This is especially the case with *poil*. Thus, 'Je n'en ai pas trouvé' is answered by the meaningless 'Poil au nez!' Then, 'Alors je n'ai plus voulu,' is answered by 'Poil au cu'.

We may compare the riming formulas of English nurseries, such as 'Georgie Porgie' and the London riming-words mentioned later.

*

Slang has therefore many resources to draw on in different kinds of permutation of the normal language. These however do not always suffice, and then it resorts to loans from foreign languages. These loans differ from ordinary borrowings. The latter are the consequence of the need or desire to express something which one's own language has no expression for, for example, foreign products or foreign ideas. Slang on the other hand, as has been said, operates in fields for which expressions already exist in the language, but expressions which people are disinclined to use because they are too trite. In Slang therefore they especially turn to such foreign words as have some-

[1] As if: We know it, we know it.
My fellow poet.
[2] Cp. Bauche pp. 163, 164 Jules.

thing comic or enlivening in their sound or form. Let me mention a few words from English slang whose origin is not generally known. *Oof*, meaning money, is a curtailed form of *ooftisch*, the Jewish-German or Yiddish *oof tisch = auf tisch*, 'money on the table'. *Choky* is used by English soldiers for 'prison'. It naturally reminds them of the verb *choke*, but it is a borrowing from the Hindostani *chauk*, 'shed, station'.

Finally, to make Slang-words, recourse is had to purely arbitrary original formations. In Denmark during the last twenty years a verb *pjække* has started up, meaning to shirk work, and an adjective *spy = amusing*.

After this exposition it will be easily seen that Slang in itself is fundamentally different from other kinds of language with which it is often confused. It is, for example, quite different from professional 'shop.' Every profession and trade (carpenters, bricklayers, electricians, journalists or whatever it may consist of) has a number of special technical terms and phrases which are unknown outside its own circle. But, if joiners do not understand the special terms used by printers, well, we are each of us unacquainted with the names of a number of people outside the circle in which we live. The two cases are essentially alike. It is rather different when we find that some of these trade-terms may have originally sprung up as slang and may still be felt to be Slang, or jesting expressions — for example when printers use in Danish the word *begravelse* (burial), or in German *eine leiche* (a corpse), when the compositor skips from one word in a manuscript to the same word a little lower down, or, on the other hand, the word *bryllup* (wedding), German *hochzeit*, when he has set the same word or passage twice over. Here then we get Slang within a trade-language, — a trade-slang. But the fact that one word belongs to two categories at the same time does not make the two categories identical.

Nor again is Slang identical with Vulgar Speech, even though Slang will often be avoided by fastidious speakers, who think it more refined to keep to the normal words of the language, and even though people who wish to avoid what is trite in language will often be led to seize on the very expression which the common people habitually employ in the same sense. The contrast between the two linguistic forms is wittily played on by Bernard Shaw in *Pygmalion* where the London flower-girl with her awful dialect has her pronunciation corrected by the phonetician, who however does not eradicate all her vulgarisms. When she is received into 'good society', these are considered by the young men who meet her as consciously humorous Slang, and as such are admired by them.

CHAPTER IX

MYSTICISM OF LANGUAGE

We may make a transition to the treatment of a new side of the life of language by considering one of the concepts for which many languages are richest in slang-expressions, namely *death*. Nearly all the words which properly mean to go, to go away, or can be used in slang in that sense, can be used in a transferred sense to mean 'to die'. It is so with the Danish *kradse av*, *forsvinde* etc. and with the English, *go away*, *peg out*, *cut one's stick*, *make one's bow* etc. But there are countless variants besides. In English, *turn up one's toes*, or *cock up one's toes*, *kick the bucket*,[1] *go aloft* (nautical), *cut the painter*, *slip one's cable* (also nautical), *peg out*, *hop off*, *hop the twig*, *give in*, *give up*, *take an earth bath*, *hang up the spoon*, snuff *the candle*, snuff *it*.

[1] It may be mentioned as a curiosity that in the Creole language spoken by the negroes of Tobago, 'to die' or 'to be dead' is expressed by *kekrebu*, elsewhere in the West Indies by *kickeraboo*. The word is nothing but *kick the bucket*, which the negroes heard used by English sailors. (Schuchardt, *Saramakka* p. 118).

Among French slang-words for 'to die' may be mentioned: *casser sa pipe*, *n'avoir plus mal aux dents*, *passer l'arme à gauche*, *fermer son parapluie*, *éteindre son gaz*, *faire sa malle*, *faire ses petits paquets*, *manger les pissenlits par la racine* (or, *de dessous*), *casser son cable* (cp. the English equivalent).

The World-War naturally made the soldiers think a great deal about death and slaughter, and led to their using different expressions for these ideas. C. Alphonso Smith [1] writes: '*Got it* is the only way doughboys (soldiers) ever refer to being killed in battle. One never hears them mention the words "dead" or "killed". (p. 79). On p. 84 he discusses the expression *gone West* for the same idea. So M'Knight [2] speaks of it as an outcome of 'the spirit of army life' that 'the serious was made light of by such expressions as *go West*, *click it*, *push up the daisies*, for "die", and *bumped off*, *knocked off* for "killed".'

Here however the author has hardly seized the real or deepest motive for these circumlocutions. It was not in order to make light of what was serious that the soldiers used these words, but rather out of an ingrained fear of the right word, a belief, that is, in a more or less supernatural power immanent in the word itself. Even in ordinary peaceful life we are not inclined to use these blunt words of the dead, when our own dear ones are in question: we say *he has gone from us*, or *he has passed away*. We are

[1] *New Words Self-defined*, New York, 1920.
[2] *English Words and their Background*, New York and London, 1923, p. 277.

afraid of the word, like the English child whom Lady Glenconner tells of who said: ' "I think it is the name that is so frightening, Moth'; I dont like to say it, it is so terrible. Death", he shuddered as he lay in bed, "I wish it wasn't called that! I dont think I should mind it so much if it were called Hig." ' Here of course the child deceives himself. If he had belonged to a linguistic community in which *Hig* was the plain unadorned name for death, the three sounds would of course have produced the same horror in his mind as the three sounds which now in his native language make up the word *death*.

I may also mention here an English slang-expression which sprang up in the War, when English soldiers in France came into contact with French words which they only partially understood. Out of 'il n'y a plus', they seized on the syllables 'na poo, na pooh', and used them as an exclamation with the meaning, 'All over.'

'You say "Na pooh" when you push away your plate after dinner. It also means, "Not likely!" or "Nothing doing!" By a further development it has come to mean "done for", "finished", and in extreme cases, "dead". "Poor Billy got na-poohed by a rifle grenade yesterday," says one mourner to another.'[1] Another euphemism for the same idea gives the English novelist, Miss Rose Macaulay, occasion for the witty remark, that 'it's a queer thing how 'fallen' in the masculine means killed in the war, and in the feminine, given over to a particular kind of vice'.[2] In both

---

[1] Ian Hay, *The first hundred thousand* p. 302. Cp. C. Alphonso Smith, p. 125 ff.

[2] *Potterism,* p. 59.

expressions one may assuredly see an outcome of the fear of the naked word, an after-echo of the view held by savage tribes that a name is something with a real existence outside humanity, something possessing power, so that the way to escape evil consequences is not to use the plain word for anything bad or dangerous.

We have then here a different motive for avoiding the simple, normal word than that which we saw in slang. There it was disinclination to use something that had lost all colour: here an expression is avoided from a certain fear, a more or less religious dread, of bringing on oneself woeful consequences by naming a name or a word which for one reason or another has become *taboo*. This *tabu*, *tapu*, *taboo* is a Polynesian word for what is holy, mystically untouchable: it may be an *object* which one dare not touch or look at, but it may also be a *word* which one dare not utter. In place of the taboo'd word one uses another. This harmless word that has been substituted, the Polynesians call *noa*.

We shall never thoroughly understand the nature of language, if we take as our starting point the sober attitude of the scientifically-trained man of today, who regards the words he uses as means for communicating, or maybe further developing, thought. To children and savages a word is something very different. To them, there is something magical or mystical in a name. It is something that has power over things and is bound up with them in a far more intimate manner than we are wont to imagine. This view may begin very early in the child's life. The child that notices that it does

not get anything if it does not ask for it nicely, but
that its parents at once fulfil its wishes when it says
'water, please', rejoices in the magical power he has
come to possess by the utterance of these syllables.
As Sully expresses it: 'children regard names as objective realities mysteriously bound up with the things,
and, in a manner, necessary to them. A nameless
object is, for a child, something incomplete — almost
uncanny', [1] and 'the childish tendency to "reify" the
name, that is, to regard it as part of the real thing
itself, instead of something extraneous and arbitrarily
attached to it'. [2]

We meet similar conceptions among the savage
tribes of very different parts of the globe. [3] Knud
Rasmussen several times describes the Greenland-
ers' view of the Name as something self-existent:
'They divide a person into a soul, a body, and a
name .... The name is a soul, with which a
certain stock of vital power and dexterity is bound
up. A person who is named after a dead man, in-
herits his qualities, and the dead man is not at rest,
his life's-soul cannot pass to the land of the dead, until a child has been named after him. Connected with
this view is the fear of mentioning a dead man's name,
before a child has received it, lest the man should
thus lose some part of its virtue. After the death of the
body, the name takes up its abode in a pregnant

---

[1] *Nineteenth Century* Nov. 1891 p. 739.

[2] *The Human Mind,* 1892, p. 312.

[3] The magical power of the Name is treated psychologically
in C. K. Ogden and I. A. Richards' *The Meaning of Meaning*
(London 1923).

woman, and keeps her inwardly pure during her pregnancy; then it is born with the child'.[1]

Connected with such superstitious conceptions are the customs found under varying forms in many other parts of the world for perpetuating a man's name. Some of the facts were brought to light by Gustav Storm, who succeeded in drawing from them some interesting conclusions in regard to Scandinavian history in the Middle Ages. A collection of other material is to be found, *e. g.* in Feilberg's Jutland Dictionary under the word 'navn' [name], where many references are given. The main principle in old times was that a child was called after that relative, recently dead, whose soul and power and luck it was desired that the child should inherit, on the supposition that these things would come to the child with the name. Long after this conception had passed, it lived on in customs connected with the naming of children. So in many places there was a disinclination to give a child its father's name, unless the latter had died before the child's birth, in which case the child took his name almost as a matter of course. So, children were named much more frequently after dead grandparents than after living ones. Many other peculiar points with regard to the naming of children find a simple explanation, when the ideas of a primitive race on the nature and vital significance of the name are taken into account.

Many primitive peoples are afraid of mentioning their name to strangers: it is a part of their being, and they do not wish others to get power over them

---

[1] *Nye mennesker*, pp. 121, 130: *Grønland*, p. 124.

by knowing their names (Niceforo GA. p. 208 f.). The Sakalava's in Madagascar are not allowed to communicate to strangers either their own name or the name of their village, for fear the strangers should make a mischievous use of it. (Walen).

In some Australian tribes everyone has two names: — a general name, and a special name only known to members of his totem-group (Spencer and Gillen). The Araukans carefully conceal their personal-name from strangers: in their presence they are called by their family-name. Near Tyer's Lake in Victoria the natives mention no one by his name, but call him brother or cousin, or use designations like the left-handed one, the little fool (Lefébure).

In South Italy a man who is suspected of being a 'jettatore', having the 'evil eye', is never spoken of by name, but only as 'he who cannot be named' or 'Mr. . . . ., let us not name him' It is thought that the mere naming of the 'jettatore' brings ill-luck, just as much as seeing or touching him. (Niceforo G A 210.)

In popular belief as reflected in fairy-tales, songs, and traditional legends, we find again and again the idea that knowledge of the name of a person or thing gives one power over the person or the thing. One example must suffice. When St. Lawrence was building the cathedral at Lund, he received supernatural assistance from a goblin ('trold') who by way of reward was to have the saint's two eyes unless the latter could name his name. When the church was nearly finished, Lawrence heard a woman on a little hill outside the town hush her weeping children with the promise that their father Finn was soon coming with gifts for them. Lawrence could therefore hurl the name at the goblin, who on the instant lost his power and was turned to stone. [1]

A similar magical power, according to popular belief, lies in various formulas, which, if spoken or merely written, are powerful enough to keep anything evil away, to cure sickness, bring good to him who knows them and applies them, and cause harm to his enemy. Such formulas are found in all countries: they often contain words or fragments of words which are not intelligible. Here I will only bring evidence from Greenland where, according to Knud Rasmussen, [2] one finds charms with old untranslatable, apparently meaningless, words which old men have dreamt. 'They are handed on from generation to generation. Everyone regards them as of great value, but he is not allowed to impart them till he feels the approach of death'.

It is also well-known what great magical importance has been attached in many places to words or letters, scratched or written in different ways on different objects, to give the writer power over persons or things. The runes were originally not so much means of communications as charms. One of the most important passages for the understanding of the subject is the stanzas woven into the songs about Sigurd in the Edda, in which it is said:

[1] Connected with this is the great mystical importance assigned in various poems of the Edda (e. g. Vafþrúþnismál, and especially Alvismál) to knowledge of names, especially of the names of gods and things connected with the gods.

[2] *Grønland* p. 123.

Winning-runes learn, if thou longest to win,
  And the runes on thy sword-hilt write;
Some on the furrow, and some on the flat,
  And twice thou shall call on Tyr.

Ale runes learn, that with lies the wife
  Of another betray not thy trust;
On the horn thou shalt write, and the backs of thy hands,
  And Need (N) shalt mark on thy nails.

Birth-runes learn, if help thou wilt lend,
  The babe from the mother to bring.

And thus it goes on with sea-runes, medicinal runes, and runes of wisdom.

Speech-runes learn, that none may seek
  To answer harm with hate . . . .

Thought-runes learn, if all shall think
  Thou art keenest minded of men. [1]

But about charms and similar magical expedients in other countries, others are far more competent to speak than I.

A consequence of the primitive view of the close mystical connexion between name and thing is the importance often attached to a man's changing his name when he becomes a ruling sovereign. His power and authority is now different from what it was before, he has become a different man, and this is expressed by his taking a new name, [2] often with a solemn ceremonial. Again, not unfrequently, a young man changes his name, when with solemn religious ceremonies he

[1] *Sigrdrifomál* 6 ff., transl. by H. A. Bellows, New York 1923.
[2] For the effect of this custom on the general vocabulary, see below.

is formally received into the body of grown-up men
which often takes place only after hard probation ac-
companied by downright torture.

Of somewhat similar character is the custom that
a woman when she enters the married state takes her
husband's surname, in token that she now leaves the
circle of her original family and is received into a
new one. It is well known that many women of the
Woman's Movement have of late years protested
against this custom, reading in it an implication that
by the change of name the married woman is some-
how stamped as the property of her husband, and
surrenders her innermost nature as a self-existing individual. It would follow from this, though the consequence is not generally drawn, that it is also de-
grading to a child to take his father's surname, since
it is thereby stamped as belonging to a particular
family or 'gens'.

In many countries it is not persons merely who
change their name, towns do so also. And this change
of name is not a mere shifting of a label: it is supposed to be of great symbolical importance to the life
of the nation. It betokened a new epoch in the national life of the Japanese when their capital gave up
its ancient name *Yeddo*, and took the new name
Tokyo, meaning 'the eastern residence'. And elsewhere on the earth's surface capitals change their
name and deep importance is attached to the change.
St. Petersburgh became Petrograd, and has now become Leningrad: Christiania has become Oslo.

In the Anemerina tribes of Madagascar the King
changes his name on his coronation-day; for instance,

Rabodo became Ranavalona I, Rakoto called himself
Radama II. But at the same time all names of things
or beings, which resemble the King's new name, dis-
appear from the ordinary vocabulary. When Queen
Rasoherina came to the throne, the word *soherina*
(silkworm) was forbidden, and replaced by *zana dandy*,
which means, 'silk's child'. If the prince takes the name
Andriamambra, the word *mambra* (crocodile) in the
ordinary language must be replaced by *voay*: if he
calls himself *Ramboa*, the word *amboa* (dog) must
vanish, and people must say *fandroaka* (the hunter) or
famovo (the barker).[1] Similar customs are found in
many other parts of the world.

According to W. Thalbitzer,[2] 'The principal cause
of the difference between East and West Greenlandic
is the religious taboo-custom that made it compulsory
to alter a word whenever a person died who bore the
same word as a name; for the name of the deceased
must never be spoken unless before his death his
name had been given to a person still alive, and even
then it was better not to mention the name. The
new word was formed by derivation from another stem
with a similar meaning, or that meant something that
could be used as a metaphoric paraphrasing of the
word tabooed. When the two men *Umiaq* and *Inik*
died, their names, that were common words for
"women's boat" and "human being", were tabooed,
and replaced with *Aawtarit* and *Taaq*, the former a
paraphrase of "women's boat", meaning "a means of

---

[1] Sibree; Niceforo G A p. 240; Frazer, *Golden Bough* III p. 378.
[2] *The Ammassalik Eskimo* in *Meddel. fra Grønland* XL 1923,
p. 115.

moving by boat from the winter residence to the sum-
mer place", the latter meaning literally 'a shadow' . .
In other cases obsolete words, or words of the sacred
language of the priests (angakkut) seem to have been
made use of'.

In the same work, p. 159, he is speaking of native
Greenland poets who are famous in their lifetime,
but 'the death of the poet or artist casts the fatal
shade of taboo over his name, which it is forbidden
to mention, and therefore everlasting fame does not
fall to the lot of the classical product of any Eskimo
poet'.

The Todas of Southern India have very similar
conceptions and customs. The late Dr. W. H. R.
Rivers writes[1]: 'If two men have the same name,
and one of the two should die, the other man would
change his name, since the taboo on the name of the
dead would prevent people from uttering the name of
the living . . . two men named *Matowan* . . . one
died, and the other changed his name to *Imokhvan*
. . . . This change of name may also be effected even
when there is only a similarity between the two names
. . . when *Oners* . . . died, *Einers* changed his name
to *Tokulvan* . . . When a man is ill, change of name
is sometimes recommended by the diviner, but this is
not often done . . . A man may not utter the names
of his mother's brother, his grandfather and grand-
mother, his wife's mother, and of the man from whom
he has received his wife, who is usually the wife's
father. The names of the above are tabooed in life,
while after death the restrictions are still wider, and it

[1] *The Todas* p. 625 f.

is forbidden to utter the name of any dead elder relative, while the names of the dead are in any case only said reluctantly . . . The Todas dislike uttering their own names, and a Toda, when asked for his name, would often request another man to give it'. On the other hand there is no taboo-prohibition among the Todas against uttering 'the names of the objects which correspond to the names of the dead, or to parts of their names'.

The common prohibition of uttering the dead man's name is due according to Niceforo (G A p. 245) to the belief that the dead man is included in the class of untouchable (holy or unclean) beings which must not be touched without observing the very strictest precautions: the dead man's name and the dead man himself making up only one single being.

Often again people dare not mention the names of various gods, devils, or good and evil spirits, as by doing so they may bring upon themselves the wrath of the invisible powers. The best known case is *Jehovah (Jahveh)*, whom the Jews dared not name and so substituted *Adonai*, 'the lord'. But a corresponding prohibition and fear is found in many places. We have indeed something of it in our European forms of oath, as when we Danes instead of swearing by '*guds død og pine*' ('God's death and passion') are content to say *død og pine*. So in English the word God is either shortened as in the obsolete oath *drot*, *drat* from *God rot*, or transformed to *gosh, Gad, cock, bob, Great Scott, gog, gough, gum, golly, gummy, dad (bedad, adad)*, not to speak of *goodness*, and similar harmless substitutes. In German, to take an example, they have *Pott* for *Gott* (*Potts slapperment* for *Gottes sa-krament*), in French *bleu* in *morbleu* from *mort Dieu*, etc. People are shy again about naming the devil (*djævelen*, *fanden*, in Danish) and to avoid the proper name say *den onde*, 'the evil one', or the like.

(Both the above Danish names for devil are origin-ally noa-names: *diabolos*, properly, the calumniator, the enemy, and *fanden*, either a transformation of *fjenden*, the enemy, or, more probably, the 'tempter', from the verb which we have in Old English, *fandian*, to prove, tempt.)

The ancient Romans believed that their city had a special god, whose name however was so holy that it was a capital offence to disclose it, and it was even forbidden, as Plutarch tells us, to inquire into the god's sex. The city itself had also a secret holy name, the mention of which involved the punishment of death. As an illustration drawn from quite modern times I may quote what Vambéry[1] relates of his Jewish-orthodox home in Hungary, where to avoid mention of the Christian cross, *(kreuz)*, they had to call the coin *kreuzer* a *schmeitzer*.

Similar ideas of the nature of a name and of the mystical power of a word are at the bottom of a multitude of superstitions the whole world over. Many of these are as much alive as ever among the peasantry, though many have been driven out in civilized coun-tries during the last few centuries, or perhaps, actu-ally, only within the last few decads. A mass of illu-strations of name-superstitions and word-taboo drawn from many countries and languages is collected in Kr.

[1] *Story of my Struggles*, p. 29.

Nyrop's very able early work *Navnets magt* [1] and in the third volume of Sir J. G. Frazer's *Golden Bough*.

Animals which people for some reason or other are afraid of, they dare not call by their right names, either at all or at certain seasons, especially the great annual festivals. So the wolf (ulven) is (or was till recently) called *gråben* (the 'gray-legged'), the field-mouse (markmusen) is called *blakke*, the weasel (væselen) is called *den kønne* ('the pretty one'), rats (rotterne) are called *de store* ('the big ones'), *de store teder* (a word otherwise unknown), or *de langrumpede* ('the longtailed ones'), *ukær*, *utøj* ('vermin'); mice (musene) are called *de sma gra* ('the little gray ones'), *tederne* or *de små teder*.

On Sejer Island, between Christmas and the New Year one must not speak of 'rotter eller mus, lopper eller lus' ('rats or mice, fleas or lice') or they breed prolifically. In Jutland children used to be told: you mustn't say *lus* (lice), you must say *basser*, ('big ones'), or there will be too many of them. Prohibitions of this sort are found by the hundred in all countries.

Ivar Aasen (*Ordbog*, p. 976) tells us of cases of name-taboo in which certain names might not be uttered by fishermen while they were at sea. And when Jakob Jakobsen went to Shetland to look for traces there of the old Norse language, he only began to reap a rich harvest after he had got on such friendly terms with the inhabitants as to be allowed to accompany them when they went fishing. He then discovered that, along with the English-Scottish names

[1] In *Mindre afhandlinger udg. af det filologisk-historiske samfund*, København, 1887.

for fish and tackle which they used every day, they had a whole set of other names to which superstitious ideas were attached, and which for the most part were the old Norwegian or Old Norse names, still living a strange hidden life. Many of them are even among the words mentioned in Snorre's Edda as specially poetical. [1]

He found also peculiar place-names of 'Pictish' (rather, Cymric) origin, which were preserved as 'taboo-names' for certain landmarks by help of which the fishermen found their fishing-grounds. On dry land these places had Norse names (*Danske Studier* 1919, p. 147).

It is now coming to be generally recognized by linguistic investigators that such name-taboo's have had a great influence on the evolution of vocabulary. So in many places the proper name for the 'bear' has been lost. In Lapland people are so much afraid of its killing the cattle that they do not call it by its usual name *guouzhja*, but say *moedda-aigja*, which means 'grandpapa with the skin coat' (Leem, Nyrop, p. 30): other names also are given. In Siberia the Yakuts call the bear Our lord, famous old man, good father, and so on. This helps us to understand how the old Aryan name for the bear, which we know from the Gk. *arktos*, Sk. *rkṣah*, Zend *aršo*, Lat. *ursus*, Erse *art*, etc., has entirely disappeared in a number of related languages, and has been replaced by different circumlocutions: Slavonic *medvĕdĭ*, Russian *medvĕd*, which originally means 'honey-eater',

[1] J. Jakobsen, *Det norrøne sprog på Shetland* (København 1897 pp. 27, 82 ff.)

Lithuanian *lokys*, which probably means 'the sweet-toothed', and the Danish *bjørn*, Germ. *bär*, Engl. *bear*, which means 'the brown'.

In the same way in various languages the old names for snakes have been lost, and replaced by such words as Lat. *serpens*, the creeper. The Danish *slange*, Germ. *schlange*, probably originally meant the same: cp. the O.H.G. verb *slingan*, to twist, creep; in other languages we have words which mean 'earthly' or 'disgusting'. Meillet, who has treated of these taboo's, reminds us that on a Malay island near Sumatra it is forbidden to speak of eyes in the hunting season and thinks that this may throw light on the strange fact that in our family of languages the words for 'eye', though related, do not exactly correspond when one passes from one language to another. It is possible that, to avoid the old word, people speaking certain languages were content to use a slightly altered form, while in Irish it was replaced by a word meaning 'sun': *súel*. (LH. 281 ff.) Kretschmer [1] is certainly right in saying that the reason why the generally-used Ancient Greek names for bread and wine, *ártos* and *oînos*, have disappeared from colloquial modern Greek, where they are replaced by *psomí* and *krasí*, is that the words had become holy by being used in connexion with the Sacrament of the Lord's Supper, just as in German *abendmal* has been lost in profane use, and is replaced by *abendessen*, *abendmahlzeit*, and in Austria by *nachtmahl*. (In Danish, probably for the same reason *nadver* (supper, i. e. the Lords Supper) has gone out of use as the name of a meal except in some dialects.)

[1] Gercke and Norden, *Einleit. i. d. Altert.* I p. 502.

Kretschmer mentions also that the Latin *verbum* has been lost in all the Romance vernaculars except Roumanian *(vorbă)*, because it had been consecrated ('gewehrt') by its religious application to the Word of God. It is replaced by *parabola*, French *parole*.

In a treatise which has just appeared,[1] J. Vendryes maintains that certain small changes in words, otherwise unexplainable, may be due to taboo: such transpositions of sounds, for example, as give us two words in Gothic for 'deaf': *bauþs* and *daufs*, and two forms for 'she-goat': *dighā (whence the OHG. *ziga*, NHG. *ziege*) and **ghaido-* (whence OHG. *geiz*, Goth. *gaits*, Eng. *goat*, Dan. *ged*). In other cases it is the initial consonant which is changed: we have *d* in the Lat. *dingua*, later *lingua*, Goth. *tuggo*, E. *tongue*, and on the other hand *t* in Irish *tenge*. He mentions some adjectives denoting colour, in which the initial sounds change in a remarkable manner. It is perhaps doubtful if all the words he names can be explained in this way, but the thought of taboo at any rate opens wider vistas, and may certainly come to play a great part in future etymological investigations. It is well known that hunters have special names for the different part of the body of the animals hunted. The hare's tail has in Danish a particular name *blommen* or *blomsten*, the fox's *lunten*: the legs of the quadrupeds are called *løbene*: the male hare is called *ramler*, the female *sætter* etc. There is no doubt that these special designations are connected with ancient superstition. It brings bad luck in the chase if the hunter is not careful to observe precisely the special words re-

[1] In *Mélanges offerts à Ch. Andler.*

quired in the case of each animal. I do not know whether the same is true of the corresponding terms used by English sportsmen, *brush* = fox's tail, *mask* = fox's face, *pad* = fox's foot.

Finally, we have the special 'women's language', found in many different parts of the world Often it merely includes a number of expressions specially used by women (or by women and children). But often it also embraces special grammatical forms or customary pronunciations; but all these peculiarities are largely or entirely dependent on old beliefs, according to which certain words and expressions are taboo for certain persons and must therefore be replaced by other words, by noa-words. [1]

It has often been remarked how tenaciously savage races cling to everything that is traditional: how, for example, they fashion and employ their tools without deviating a hair's breadth from the manner in which their ancestors did so before them. This conservatism has rightly been recognized [2] as resulting from an active faith in the things' possessing mystical properties, the potency of which depended on the objects' forms, so that by making the least change in them one would lose one's power over them. Mysterious dangers were threatened if anything was changed. For similar reasons primitive races cling with equal tenacity to their inherited language. Of course mutations of language to a great degree elude human observation, and it therefore happens that without the natives detecting it, their language does alter little by

[1] See my *Language* Chap. XVI.
[2] See Lévy-Bruhl FM p. 35.

little with the daily use made of it and with its transmission to new generations. But, so far as they can, they see to it strictly that nothing shall be changed, (apart from the case where a belief in the mystical power of the name actually demands the adoption of new words) and the most scrupulous watch is kept that there should be no change in the holy forms of religious worship and ceremonial hymns. It is owing to this careful watch over the old traditional sounds of words that the old Vedic hymns of the Indians have been orally preserved with such great fidelity that we are acquainted with their forms and pronunciation to the minutest detail. According to Sylvain Lévy, the old Vedic language was to such an extent an exclusively religious language, that it was not till the arrival of conquerors from without who were strange to Indian tradition that people dared to employ Sanskrit in profane literature.

While, then, in discussing the fear of mystical effects from the use of one word instead of another, we spoke, from our civilized standpoint, of *superstition*, here, where we are speaking of keeping unchanged what one's ancestors have handed down to one, we will rather regard this as an outcome of a commendable religious feeling, closely allied to the warm feeling with which each one of us conceives his own native language as a holy national inheritance.

CHAPTER X

OTHER ECCENTRICITIES OF LANGUAGE

In most of what we say, there is, or ought to be, some meaning. But there are departments of language which have no meaning, and never have had. Human beings — let us rather say, *some* human beings — have always found pleasure in playing with long combinations of syllables to which no meaning, or no complete meaning, is attached. It is so with many children, it is so with the so-called glossolalists or speakers with tongues, who give a religious significance to meaningless, unintelligible words and sentences which are not words or sentences at all; it is so with the Dadaists;[1] it is so, to come to a higher sphere, with Rabelais, who amuses himself by collocating long strings of more or less coarse, more or less meaningless words, which are often only comic by reason of their sound. In popular fairy-stories one often encounters the most extraordinary names, which by their mere sound have tickled the popular fancy.[2]

[1] Cf. A. Schinz in *Smith Coll. Studies*, Oct. 1923.
[2] For references see Feilberg *Ordbog* II p. 675 b.

The same thing is seen on a large scale in songs and in poetry generally. It is specially manifest in the countless refrains, which, analysed in the light of reason, hardly mean anything at all, but which by their mere sound produce an impression, and either call up an emotion, or reinforce the emotion called up by the content of the song. [1] When we have such great difficulty in understanding the old religious hymns of various countries that philologists have often given them up as insoluble, the reason, as Meillet insists, does not entirely lie in the archaic forms of the language, in which they are written, and our ignorance of many of the allusions they contain: 'We must also take into consideration that the authors have not as a rule, striven to be easily intelligible, but on the contrary have found a pleasure in being obscure and eccentric, and in expressing themselves in a non-natural manner. If the gâthâ's of the Avesta are more than unintelligible, it is because the writers wilfully made them so, the arrangements of words are unnatural. . . . . The Vedic hymns and the song of the Arval Brethren of Rome are also intentionally obscure . . . The poets must follow custom and usage, and allow their language to get very remote from the speech of every day they are addressing a public which is trained to understand this special dialect, and is besides content to admire what it does not entirely understand'. [2]

Thalbitzer brings evidence of just the same thing in the poetry of East Greenland: and it is so all over

---

[1] On such refrains in the songs of uncivilized people, see, among others, Bücher AR p. 303.

[2] Gr pp. 127, 140.

the world. A number of unintelligible words and phrases are used in primitive poetry, everywhere. In the poems changes are made even in particular sounds. In the Japanese No-drama there are a whole set of artificial articulations, nasalizing, straining of muscles, hoarse tones of voice, an inclination to the making of cacuminal sounds, a prolonged delivery of each syllable taken separately, falsetto-notes which go specially high at every second or third syllable, etc.[1] Similar customs of Indians and Papuans are described by E. Sapir.[2]

In the poetry of the old Norsemen we again find a liking for meaningless sounds. Take the names for dwarfs in the Snorra Edda:

Nýi ok Niði,
Norðri, Suðri,
Austri, Vestri,
Alþjófr, Dvalinn,
Nár ok Náinn,
Nípingr, Dáinn,
Bífurr, Bǫfurr,
Bǫmburr, Nóri,
Óri, Ónarr,
Óinn, Mjǫðvitnir,
Viggr ok Gandálfr,
Vindálfr, Þorinn,
Fíli, Kíli,
Fundinn, Váli,
Þrór, Þróinn,

---

[1] Edwards, *Ét. phon. de la langue japonaise*, p. 78.
[2] *Abnormal types of Speech in Nootka*, p. 11 ff.

Þekkr, Litr ok Vitr,
Nýr, Nýráðr,
Rekkr, Rádsviðr.

Some of these names recall well-known words. Most of them however are certainly empty sounds, but, as such of great effect.

Odin himself gives his many names on this wise:

Hétumk [I am called] Grímr
ok Gangleri,
Herjann, Hjálmberı,
Þekkr, Þriði,
Þuðr, Uðr,
Helblindi, Hárr,
Saðr, Svipall,
Sanngetall,
Herteitr, Hnikarr,
Bileygr, Báleygr,
Bǫlverkr, Fjǫlnir,
Grimnir, Glapsviðr, Fjǫlsviðr,
Síðhǫttr, Siðskeggr,
Sigfǫðr, Hnikuðr,
Alfǫðr, Atríðr, Farmatýr,
Óski, Ómi,
Jafnhárr, Biflindi,
Gǫndlir, Hárbarðr,
Sviðurr, Sviðrir,
Jálkr, Kjalarr, Viðurr,
Þrór, Yggr, Þundr,
Vakr, Skilfingr,
Váfuðr, Hroptatýr,
Gautr, Veratýr.

Here again we have a seemingly confused mixture of names for Odin known to us from other sources, words with full meaning ('broadhat, broadbeard', etc.), and, finally, no few that are mere empty names, unconnected with anything known, but effective as mere sounds.

I will quote one more list of names, in this case names for witches:

> Grior ok Gnissa,
> Gryla, Brýja,
> Glumra, Geitla,
> Grima ok Bakrauf,
> Guma, Gestilja,
> Grottintanna,
> Gjalp, Hyrrokkin,
> Hengikepta,
> Gneip ok Gnepja,
> Geysa, Hála,
> Horn ok Hrúga,
> Harðgreip, Forað,
> Hryggða, Hveðra,
> ok Holgabrúðr,
> Hrímgerðr, Hæra,
> Herkja, Fála,
> Imð, Járnsaxa,
> Íma, Fjolvor,
> Morn, Íviðja,
> Ámgerðr, Simul,
> Sívor, Skríkja,
> Sveipinfalda.

So it goes on, page after page. Editors treat these rigmaroles like naughty children and make them stand

in the corner. They consider them to be spurious.
But why should they not be genuine? They certainly
amused the old Norsemen, and interested Snorri who
found them worth taking down. Apart from their
mere sound, which to some extent may be pleasing
even to us, they doubtless to the Norsemen had a
mystical, magical, half-religious, or entirely religious,
value. It was strings of sounds of this sort which
they used to conjure the evil spirits, and master the
hidden powers of nature.

Karl Bücher in his studies on the origin of poetry
attaches great weight to the fact that, in the songs of
many savage tribes, the natural rhythm of the words,
as used in everyday speech, is altered and adapted to
the ends of poetry. He mentions,[1] for example, that
the Andaman Islanders change and shorten the words
in their language for the sake of rhythm to such a
point that it may almost be said that they have a
special poetical language. According to another ob-
server, says Bücher, it often happens that the composer of a new song has first to instruct the singers
and the audience in ordinary language as to what the
song means. Eyre says similarly of Central Australia that
many natives are not able to throw light on the meaning
of the songs of their own native place, and that it is
his belief that the explanations they give are as a rule
very incomplete, inasmuch as they seem to lay more
weight on the measure and the length of the syllables
than on the meaning. Bücher is therefore of opinion
that the rhythm of songs was not originally governed
by the particular language, but by the rhythm of the

[1] AR p. 296.

work on which the singers were engaged. Every single sort of work, he says, has its special 'time', and that decides the rhythm of the accompanying song. The actual rhythm of conversation makes such a slight impression on the ear that it cannot have produced the strongly marked rhythms of the songs and poems, with their numbering of the strong syllables and their regular separating of them by distinct intervals. This however is characteristic of many different kinds of work, which call for regularly recurring movements of the muscles and limbs. "Iambi and trochees are stamping measures, one foot that treads softly and one that treads firmly: the spondee is a striking-measure which may be everywhere easily recognized when the two hands are clapped in musical time: the dactyl and the anapæst are hammering-measures, which may be heard any day in any village smithy where the smiths let two short blows precede, or follow, the strong blow on the glowing iron: the smith calls it 'making the hammer sing'. Finally, if it is desired to go further, we may hear the three pæonic feet in every threshing-floor where the corn is being threshed, or in the streets where the paviours are working with their rammers'. By this, however, he only means to throw out hints, for these metrical forms may have originated with other kinds of work.

Whatever may be the explanation, this much is certain, that in many languages, perhaps in most, even those of so-called primitive tribes, we find special features developed in the language of poetry. It is distinguished by strongly marked rhythms, and often by other sound-effetcs (initial rime, final rime). It is often full of unintelligible words, and is marked off in other ways from the prose-language used day by day. Often it stands in close connexion with, or has been developed in association with, religious rituals, and it uses all possible means to appeal in a marked degree to the emotional element in human beings, to that which lies too deep for ordinary words, and is so far unspeakable that ordinary language cannot serve its purpose, while there is still a desire to express it in words. Even in our civilized times when many of the features emphasized in this chapter have vanished from the language even of poetry, when poetic language has also been notably rationalized, so that one expects from a poem, not merely emotions and moods, but also intuition and richness of thought, — even now, Poetry is in many ways distinguished from Prose. As Ste. Beuve says: 'La poésie ne consiste pas à tout dire, mais à tout faire rêver'.

*

Among savage tribes in many different regions one finds that a secret language is employed at the reception of youths into the community of grown men. [1] We see here something akin to the secret religious languages which priests, sorcerers and medicine-men often use in their conjurations of spirits, for example among the Angakoks of Greenland. In many cases it is not easy to draw the line between these languages and the special holy languages, which for the most part are old forms of the tribe's natural language, kept alive artificially in the holy hymns and in connexion with rituals of different sorts. The common

[1] Meinhof, MSA., p. 126.

herd understands either not at all, or only dimly, what is said, intoned, or sung, on such occasions. But its very unintelligibility lends to the spoken words a kind of mystical glamour, with the result that a magical virtue is attributed to them greater than any enjoyed by ordinary words. And the priests know how to exploit the advantage they have in being possessed of the language of the very God or Gods; it serves them to strengthen their power over the laity. There is still a little of this to be seen even in Denmark, where the priests spout some strange words which many people only dimly understand, — such as *miskundhed*, *forsage*, *forfordele*, *overantvorde* etc. But this is nothing to what is found in Catholic countries, where most of the service is given in the holy Latin language. In Russia, similarly, the old Ecclesiastical-Slavonic language is used in the church-service, of which many people are only able to pick up a little here and there, often perhaps no more than to know that, whenever the words *boze moi* (my God) come, they must cross themselves.

Apart from the use made of it by the church Latin serves as a language of concealment. In earlier times it was much used for this purpose by the learned classes, even down to Holberg's Per the parish clerk, who would not part with his Latin for a hundred dollars. This use is nowadays best preserved among doctors, for whom it may often be an advantage by a sick-bed to be able to speak of *mors* without the patient's perhaps understanding that his own approaching death is in question, and to mention diseases and parts of the body which one is not disposed to mention without their Latin names. Molière can be called to witness that this use of the mystical Latin Language was not, in his time, quite exempt from humbug. But more than two hundred years after his death prescriptions must still be written in Latin in all the Western-European countries, so strong is Conservatism, and so great is the nimbus which still crowns that dead language as a language of concealment. [1]

Artificial languages of concealment may spring up anywhere where a larger or smaller group of people has an interest in being able to talk so that others may not understand what is being said. There may be all sorts of different reasons for this secrecy, and the extent to which the concealing process is carried may also vary very considerably. A word or sign mutually agreed upon may be the starting point of a hidden-language. In the great shops at Rome the shop-assistants, when they suspect the presence of a thief among the customers, will come out with some sentence or other in which the numerals *two* and *ten* are worked in. The meaning is that the other shall have his two (eyes) turned to the customer's ten (fingers), the customer himself not understanding this meaning. [2] In the same way in English shops they say (or used to say) 'two upon ten', when attention was to be directed to a suspected customer. This became changed to 'two pun' ten', and the question came to run (still more unintelligibly for the uniniated): 'Has that two pun' (pound) ten matter ever been settled?'

[1] On the fight to use French instead of Latin as the language of doctors and druggists, see Vossler FK p. 241 ff. and Brunot as quoted by him.

[2] Niceforo GA p. 134.

or a note with £ 2. 10 upon it was handed to the salesman. Another way of indicating the same thing was to ask aloud: 'Has Mr. Sharp come in yet?'

The most wide-spread forms for languages of concealment are those we learnt in play in our childhood, in which an ordinary word has some syllable or other inserted in it to make it unrecognizable, so for example *arbe*-talk (where 'vil du gå din vej' ('will you go your way?') becomes 'virbe durbe gårbe dirbe vejrbe') or *p*-talk (where the same sentence becomes 'vilpil dupu gåpå dinpin vejpej'). We find in all parts of the world a number of variants of concealment-languages of this type. When first heard, they may leave you entirely at sea, but it is very easy to learn to understand them, and even to speak them fluently. In German there is one form (among others) in which *vater* becomes *vabateber*. The Dutch have two methods, corresponding exactly to the two Danish ones: *de schoone mei* becomes *depé schoopónepé meipéi*, or it has *-awi* as the inserted syllable. English forms are *M-gibberish* and *S-gibberish* in which *going out today* becomes respectively *goming mout tomdaym*, or *gosings outs tosdays:* 'hospital Greek' transposes *plenty of rain* into *renty of plain:* Winchester College has a language 'Ziph' or 'Hypernese', in which *wa* is substituted for the first consonant, and *p* or *g* is inserted in different ways. In France a similar language is called javanais, (Javanese). Even the Maoris of New Zealand have a language in which *kei te haere au ki reira* is changed to *te-kei te-i-te te-haere-te-re te-a te-u te-ki te-re-te-i-te-ra*. [1]

---

[1] For references to the literature of such languages, see Jespersen, *Die Sprache*, p. 131.

These languages of concealment when used by children are mere play, though of course they may be employed less innocently, when it becomes a question of talking so that teachers and parents may not understand some secret arrangement or the like.

More difficult forms of concealment-language are created, when, instead of changing the words of the ordinary language according to some one principle, one invents new words of one's own, or takes words from languages with which one's neighbours are not familiar. In my *Børnesprog* p. 145 I gave an account of such a so-called 'cur-language', invented by some young girls in a Danish parsonage about half a century ago. Some years ago a lady who is a Lecturer in Phonetics at University College, London, made me a present of a really large dictionary of a still more completely worked out language, invented by two English children, in which all the expressions seemed to be purely arbitrary. Such more or less developed 'comradeship-languages' are to be met with in all forms, from the mere creation of a few nicknames in a narrow circle, to quite definite languages which make everything that is said unintelligible to all outside the circle of the initiated. In many cases, as when a pair of lovers or a pair of friends, [1] who are constantly together and wish to cut themselves off from the world around, agree upon a string of names,

---

[1] Cp. 'l'argot des couples', Niceforo GA p. 104 ff. In Duhamel's novel *Deux hommes* there is a description of a close friendship between two men: 'ils élaborent patiemment un langage qui sera leur langage exclusif, que nul étranger bientôt ne comprendra tout à fait (p. 135).

this concealment-language has a very ephemeral existence, and is even forgotten by the persons concerned when the circumstances which led to its use have disappeared. In other cases, the language may have a more lasting importance.

In a fertile valley of North Italy, Valsoana near Turin, the inhabitants as a rule speak a dialect like any other Italian dialect. But no sooner do they come in contact with people from another district, whom they regard as strangers to whom they are unwilling to reveal their private affairs, than they in a kind of self-assertion talk to one another in a concealment-language which is different from their everyday dialect and which the strangers do not understand. In this language many words from thieves-language are interwoven, but othervise it is a changed form of their ordinary dialect with the last syllables of words slurred while in addition one of the arbitrarily chosen syllables, *ods*, *ads*, *ids*, *orl*, is inserted into words, different terminations *u*, *os*, *eri*, *ulji*, etc. are added, and finally words are replaced by periphrases as *mossa* ('the foaming') for wine, *molua* ('the crushed or ground') for meal, *bedsi* ('the beaked') for anvil, *ronfa* ('the snorer') for mill, *trentua* ('the three-toothed') for fork. [1]

The Todas similarly in Southern India, according to Rivers, [2] have a considerable number of expressions which they only use when Badagas or Tamils are present, wishing not to be understood except by their own people. To judge by the specimens given, the language consists mainly of long periphrastic express-

---

[1] Niceforo GA p. 163 ff.
[2] *The Todas* p. 616.

ions. Instead of the usual word for water, they say something which means 'what comes from the four teats of an old buffalo', for 'have you eaten?', 'teeth between did you throw?', for 'legs', 'walk things' etc. In other cases words are employed which are not otherwise used in the language. The ordinary word for tooth is *pars*, but in the secret language a tooth is *kâtô*.

The people to whom it is of most concern to have a language for use among themselves, which their fellow countrymen do not understand, are of course the professional lawbreakers. Concealment-languages are therefore often called 'thieves' language'. With thieves, go of course professional beggars, who in many places, especially in earlier times, formed a whole stratum of the community. They were closely bound up with one another and with professional law-breakers, as well as with other vagrants, tramps, knackers, Gipsies, etc. It was in connexion with the secret language of this people that the word *argot* was first used, and it would be good to restrict it to the concealment-language of thieves and beggars.[1] Its origin is unknown. Neither do we know what *flash*, the old English name for this sort of thieves language, comes from. On the other hand we do know that the other English word for the same thing, *cant*, is connected with the Italian *cantare*, which properly means to sing, but in thieves' language meant to talk, like the Italian derivative *canzonare* and *chanter* in French thieves' language, which is also found in Vil-

[1] An authority like L. Sainéan would however use *argot* for what is here called *slang*, and would call thieves' language *jargon*.

lón in this sense. *Cant* was especially applied in England to the whining tone affected by beggars, and was then transferred to the way of talking affected by religious hypocrites. But we find *to cante* (explained as 'to speake') and *canter* ('beggar') given as thieves-language, in 1566.

In these thieves-languages we again find those methods adopted for making words unrecognizable which we have mentioned already. In 'Germania', the concealment-language of Spanish lawbreakers, syllables are often transposed, thus *pecho* becomes *chepo*, and *vistar*, *tisvar*. Similarly criminals in Holland will use *nelefar* for *rafelen* and *regniv* for *vinger*. It is said that similar transpositions are employed by London costers, particularly when they wish to be able to mention the price of their commodities without their customers understanding them. They are supposed to say *net* for *ten*, *net evif* for *fifteen*, *net exis* for *sixteen;* and, further, *gennitraf* for *farthing*, *namow* for *woman*, *esclop* (whence *slop*) for *police*. It strikes one about these last words that they are obviously formed on the base, not of the sounds of the normal words, but of their spelling. They therefore imply some amount of book education, if not in the users of the language, at least in its inventors. Another of their methods is to use an apparently casual word that rimes with the word they would conceal, thus *Isabella* for *umbrella*, *honey* for *money*, *elephant's trunk* for *drunk*. These remind one of what was reported before of French slang. But, side by side of all this, one finds in thieves'-languages a number of peculiar expressions drawn from many different sources.

Many of the words of the old English thieves' jargon were known outside the thieves' circle. They are found, for example, in Shakespeare and his contemporary, Dekker, and later in Fielding, Ainsworth, Bulwer-Lytton, and others. Such are *bona roba* (borrowed from Italian), 'handsome girl', *bung*, 'purse', 'pocket', *fap*, 'maudlin drunk', etc. *Gourd* which is found in Shakespeare meaning 'false dice' evidently is the French argot *gourt*, a die for playing, from an adj. *gourd*, properly, 'heavy', 'pompous', but meaning in old argot, 'good'. (Sainéan *Arg. anc.* 210.) Many of these thieves' words are utterly unexplainable, as they were intended to be. The old Eng. *doss*, 'bed', 'sleep', is connected in the NED with another *doss*, 'back', from the Latin, *dorsum*. Possibly however it has nothing to do with that word, and is to be connected with the French, *dors*, *dormir*. Some old thieves' jargon words have passed into the current language, *e. g. prig*, *filch* to steal, *rum*, odd.

Some words, but obviously not very many, in thieves' jargons are borrowed from Gipsy language (Romany).

As is well-known, Romany was originally a real language. It comes from India and may be compared with any other national language of our linguistic family. The Gipsies during their wanderings have very faithfully kept the language of their home, so far as its kernel is concerned, even though they have adopted a number of borrowed words from the languages of the countries in which they have sojourned longest, from Greek, for example. Romany cannot therefore be properly compared with the artificial languages of concealment which have been discussed. It is another matter that the language, not being understood by the settled populations of the different countries through which they have passed, lends itself well to the purposes of a language of concealment, and is actually employed as such in many places, particularly in Armenia, where Gipsy expressions are used in this manner with Armenian pronunciation and with Armenian grammatical constructions. [1]

Thieves-languages, as their very definition would lead us to expect, vary very greatly according to time and place. There are a great number of Vocabularies of these languages. In English there is an old one in John Awdeley's 'The Fraternitye of Vacabondes' (1560), [2] and later ones by Grose and Pierce Egan and others. In Denmark, (where these jargons are called *Kæltringelatin, prævelikvant)*, there are lists compiled by Dorph, Dyrlund, and Mylius Erichsen; [3] in Norway there is one by Eilert Sundt. As for thieves' German, a collection of lists of words made at different dates is to be found in Kluge's great *Gaunersprachen*, of which unfortunately the second volume has never appeared.

I must here say a few words for completeness sake about *written* language-of-concealment. All the species hitherto treated, which to use a learned term might be called cryptologies, were intended for oral use. But along with them we have the so-called cryptographies, hidden ways of writing one's thoughts. The simplest forms are again found in the hands of children, who for every letter of the alphabet have a single sign, either a figure

---

[1] Meillet, LH p. 95.

[2] Edited by E. Viles and F. J. Furnivall, E. E. T. S. 1869.

[3] Different from these is that compiled by G. Brøchner-Mortensen, *Danske Studier*, 1920, p. 85 ff. which is essentially Slang.

or another letter, which constantly keeps the same value. It is naturally the easiest thing in the world, without the application of any excessive acuteness, to interpret cryptographies of this sort. It is only necessary to find out by counting which sign occurs most frequently, — that is *e*, — and to proceed partly by a purely statistical method, partly by noticing which combinations occur frequently etc. Cryptographies are also made, like the p-jargons, by inserting meaningless letters among the letters which are to be read. More complicated results are obtained by substitutions. Here the same letter does not always stand for the same letter of the word intended, but changes its value according to fixed rules, more or less ingeniously thought out. These are the systems used by diplomatists in their ciphers, which require special keys, which must be kept strictly secret and changed as often as possible to prevent discovery. But these cryptographic systems lie outside my present task.

CHAPTER XI

CONCLUSION UNIVERSAL HUMAN ELEMENTS

My main subject so far has been the linguistic cross-play of the individual and of the community to which he belongs, whether this latter be greater or smaller, the whole nation or a mere parish, or, again, the narrow circle with whom he shares some secret language. The more commonplace a person is, the more will his language bear the stamp of the community in which he lives: the more unique his nature, the more peculiarly his own will be the colouring of his language. He will not only be easily recognized by his voice, but his particular individuality will be recognized in his words and phrases, even through the medium of writing. This is what we mean when we say that such and such a person has a style of his own, and it is to such persons that Buffon's well-known saying, 'The style is the man himself', most fully applies. After hearing anyone of this kind talk, it happens again and again that when we read something that he has written, we quite involuntarily imagine that we hear the intonations of his voice in the written words. There are indeed some philologists nowadays who think that they can go further than this. They hold that, by surrendering themselves sympathetically and whole-heartedly to reading some old work, they can so catch the ring of the writer's sentences as to be able to recognize what is his genuine work and what is a later addition, and they declare that this 'analysis of the ring' may become an important instrument of investigation in textual criticism and the history of language. Other philologists take up a very sceptical or 'Wait and see' attitude on this question, and I shall say no more about it. Nor, again, shall I enter into the very wide and difficult questions of national character and the way in which it is reflected in the sounds, forms, syntax and vocabulary of the language.

I propose however to conclude my work with a very brief treatment of the question whether in the world of language — behind that endless variety to which we owe it that we have thousands of languages that are mutually unintelligible, — there is not still something common to all, something that belongs to all humanity, and is one and the same everywhere.

The distinguished German linguist, H. Schuchardt, has in recent years strongly insisted that similarities between different languages need not always depend on the languages being related to one another as French is related to Italian, but in some cases may be due to some element common to all mankind; in other words, some phenomena, instead of being 'geschichtlich verwandt' (historically related) may be 'elementarverwandt' (primordially related). His terms are perhaps not very happily chosen, but the distinction he draws is one that should be firmly kept in mind. It would perhaps be best to avoid the word 'related' altogether, as that word cannot bear the same meaning in linguistics that it bears in biology. Languages do not 'propagate' like animals, but only by a process of imitation. By saying that a French word and an Italian word are 'related', we mean that both in France and in Italy there is an unbroken chain of imitations leading back to a time when there was no demonstrable difference between the two languages, when in fact there was only one linguistic community, which afterwards split into two. Even borrowed words may be 'geschichtlich verwandt' as when Fr. *chocolat* corresponds to It. *cioccolata*, both words being originally borrowed from Mexican. On the other hand, in the expression 'elementarverwandt' the word *verwandt* ('related' as members of a family are related to one another) is used in a still looser sense, in the sense, that is, in which we may say that we find in Schopenhauer trains of thought which are 'related' to Indian philosophy. It would have been better here to use the term 'naturally common'.

When we examine languages, we do indeed find many things which imply the existence of a fundamental common nature in human beings all the world over. Some features of language are due to a common humanity: they show themselves just because the individuals who speak the languages are human beings. It is not necessary for us here to consider the extraordinarily difficult and involved question whether all mankind descend from a single pair, or whether man originated in a particular place and at a particular epoch, or whether on the other hand the human races, now so sharply distinguished from each other, had possibly each its separate origin. Nor shall I venture upon the difficult question whether all languages, if traced far enough back, are mutually related, each in its own way continuing the same primeval language, or if they must be referred to a greater or smaller number of mutually independent parent-languages. The former theory, that of the original unity of mankind, has very lately been championed with great learning and acuteness by the Italian linguist, A. Trombetti, [1] but his proofs do not seem to me to be convincing, and I think it will be better to leave the question open. Perhaps we shall never get the requisite data for deciding it: at present at any rate, we know too little to take a determined stand on one side or the other.

Let me draw attention to a subject closely related with this, on which opinions are also divided. Earlier anthropologists maintained that human civilization must have sprung up in many different places independently, and that the resemblances met with in different civilizations must depend on the likeness of human nature everywhere in combination with the likeness of the tasks which human communities had to overcome. But now many anthropologists, such as Dr. W. H. R. Rivers, who died a few years ago, and G. Elliot Smith, hold that points of likeness in different civili-

[1] *L'Unità d'Origine del Linguaggio*, Bologna, 1905: *La Glottologia*, 1922.

zations are due to borrowing (that is, to imitation). According to their view, civilization sprang up at a particular place, from whence it spread to other races. Even the old Maya civilization of Central America came from Asia. As proof of this is adduced the fact, that on stone monuments at Copan in Honduras are found figures representing elephants, while there are no elephants in America now, and no traces have been found of there having ever been elephants in America.[1] It would naturally not befit me to take a side in the controversy, but it is important to insist that in the world of *language* there is a bond of common human nature which can bring about the same or related effects in many different places where all thought of imitation or borrowing is absolutely excluded. If the effects, though analogous, show great variety, it is because often the fundamental common nature encounters different materials in the different languages in which it operates.

Among the things common to all mankind there is first of all the physiological basis. The organs of speech are in essential points formed alike in all races. The little differences which are of course found in the arching of the palate, in the size and form of the nasal chamber etc., seem to have no significance whatever. No one has succeeded in pointing out a single linguistic feature which can be ascribed to such anatomical causes. It is also shown that children of European parentage who pass their childhood among

[1] G. Elliot Smith, *Elephants and Anthropologists*, London, 1924. (I only know the review in the *Times Lit. Suppl.*, 12 June 1924).

Eskimo's in Greenland or among Bantu's in South Africa come to talk the Greenland or the Zulu language just like natives. Even the shades of difference in the pronunciation of labial sounds, which must necessarily result from the thick and protruded lips of negroes, seem to have no particular linguistic significance. On the other hand we certainly read of tribes which owing to the custom of distending the lower lip with a piece of metal as an adornment are incapable of having sounds like f and v in their language. A ring in the nose on the contrary does not prevent nasal-sounds being produced as perfectly by those who affect this fashion as by ourselves who do not require thus to add to our charms. The view that particular features of the pronunciation of Jews, or of Negroes in the Southern States of America, are due to racial peculiarities, to a particular formation of their organs of speech, is certainly erroneous. The defects come, without any doubt, from a faulty imitation of the speech of the people around them, partly under the influence of the foreign languages spoken by their parents which through them has affected their children. That this is the case, is seen by the fact that the young generation, even where there is no mixture of races, succeeds in imitating the language of the country without being affected in the least by their parents' speech.

It follows from this that it is possible to erect a science of general phonetics, which may explain the methods by which human speech-sounds are produced. The system of sounds is in the main the same, however many shades of difference may be substantiated in the course of comparing languages, their dialects, and the speech of single individuals. Further, inasmuch as the conditions governing changes in sounds in course of time, either through the transmission of the language to new generations or within the same generation, are everywhere the same, an investigator is not surprised when he finds the same historical changes of sound occurring all around in different places, which are quite independent of one another. It is possible to indicate certain general tendencies. Single consonants between vowels tend, for example to became voiced: a [k] is produced in a more forward position when it stands before a front-tongue vowel, so that it often becomes the combined sound [tʃ], as in Eng. *chin*, Swedish *kinn*, Ital. *cera*, or finally *s*, as in French *cire*: a stress-accent often has the effect that vowels in weak syllables become obscurely articulated mid-tongue sounds, or are entirely lost: the effect of the stress-accent on consonants, seen in Verner's Law in old Gothonic (Germanic), and in Eng. *of* [ɔv] from *off*, and *knowledge* from *knowleche* etc., can also be shown in many different languages, though in some it is carried through with less regularity than in others.

There are accordingly a whole series of changes of sound which linguistic inquirers are constantly meeting under the same or similar conditions in different countries and at the most different periods, while there are others which he never sees, because the articulations used in producing the two sounds are too different, — for example a change from *p* or *m* to *a*. But one never attains to more than the main lines of direction, and never to anything that can be compared with a physical law, like the law of gravitation for instance. What the linguist understands by a 'sound-law' is indeed at best only a rule without exceptions for a change of sound which has taken place at a definite time in a definite language.

It has been maintained that Maurice Grammont in his researches into dissimilation and assimilation has succeeded in establishing general laws, valid for all times and for all languages. The search after real laws, in the science of language as elsewhere, must be recognized as highly meritorious, but in my opinion it is doubtful if Grammont has succeeded in discovering anything that deserves the name of 'laws' in this sense. When he himself puts forward as the main result of his researches 'la loi du plus fort' ('the law of the strongest'), meaning, that it is the strongest sound which causes dissimilation or assimilation, it comes to nothing until we get definite rules to enable us to find out in any given case which sound *is* the strongest. But the criteria of the 'strength' of sounds are so numerous and in part mutually contradictory,[1] that they do not really help us any more than the statement, 'In a horse-race it is always the swiftest horse which comes in first', would help us to choose the right horse to bet on.

[1] Why is it that in the collocation *mn* it is sometimes the first sound which is the stronger, and sometimes the second? (Germ. *stimme*, Fr. *somme sommeil*, Engl. *damn* — Germ. *nennen*, Span. *sueño*, Ital. *sonno*)? Why in one district of Jutland is *r*, in another *n* the stronger in the combination *rn* as in *barn*, so that one parish says *bàr*, another *bàn*? Why is *t* stronger than *n* in the Icelandic *vatn*, where *n* is unvoiced, but weaker than *n* in Danish, where we have now *van* (written *vand*)?

To pass now from the outer form of words to their inner meaning, there is again so much that it is common to all mankind in mental basis, in psychological structure, that we cannot be surprised to find a number of correspondencies between languages widely apart. We shall constantly find that the authors of etymological dictionaries and treatises, when they want to establish the probability of some change of meaning, appeal to parallel cases in quite unrelated languages. There are universal laws of thought which are reflected in the laws of change of meaning (semantic laws), even if the Science of Meaning (Semantic, Semasiology, or whatever it is to be called) has not yet made much advance towards discovering them. As my space does not allow me to go deeper into the subject, I will here only take occasion to remark that in certain cases there may be something common to all mankind working in secret, even where the result turns out differently in different places. Thus we see frequently that the name attached to a broader concept is substituted for a more specific name, and this usage can establish itself even to the point that the older, wider meaning of the word may come to be quite forgotten. But here the special conditions prevailing in every particular place modify the result. So the word *korn (corn)* comes to mean barley in Bornholm and Samsø, as well as in South Norway and Sweden, rye in North Germany, oats in Westphalia, Scotland, and the North of Ireland, spelt in South Germany, wheat in England, maize in North America (cp. Russ. *žito* barley; French *froment*, Ital. *formento*, *grano* wheat). So in Bornholm, *fisk* means cod, in Samsø, flat fish (flounder) as opposed to cod. So we get different results from the same common tendency.

*

In treating linguistic questions we must never forget that men are only in part reasonable beings, and that the universal human element is also therefore largely irrational and illogical. The old Latin proverb 'fit denominatio a potiori', 'the name is given from the more potent quality', does not square with fact. Perhaps the sentence ought to be changed to 'fiat denominatio a potiori', and be considered an injunction or recommendation to anyone who has to choose a new name. But what has actually been the case with the names whose origin we can prove? Were they given in accordance with the proverb? And can we consequently in our etymological researches take it as given that the name at first denoted the most important element found in the object? This was the opinion of the elder school of linguists See, for example, Sayce P 301: 'Every name that is given is a summing-up of all attainable knowledge concerning a thing; it contains within itself the answer which man attempts to make to that ever-recurring question "Why?" and all the knowledge and experience which he can bring to bear upon it.

In a similar fashion, but perhaps in a fashion psychologically sounder, Wundt says that a thing is named after its most striking characteristic ('das auffallendste merkmal'), as, e. g. tischler (carpenter) from tisch (table). Wundt also uses the expression 'domi-

nierend' ('dominating'), but this is certainly wrong, if
by 'striking' and 'dominating' we think of that characteristic which in the long run is the most striking. The
statement is more correct if we mean by 'most strik
ing', that which at the chance moment when the thing
was named was uppermost in the speaker's consciousness, stood foremost in his thought, but this may well
be something to which he would probably give no
further importance at other times. The important thing
to the speaking human being is to get a name, i. e.
something which can be apprehended as such, and is
therefore adapted to be used again by one who has
heard it for the first time. And when once the name
is there, in many cases it will not matter a straw to
the man who uses it, whether the name was from the
beginning suitable and well chosen, or whether it is
suitable still: far more important is it to the simple
speaker of the language that he has a name which he
has found ready-made and to which his fellows attach
the same meaning as he does. It is impossible to
give a tradesman a name to suit everything that he
deals in. *Ironmongers* and *costermongers* (from *coster*,
costard, a particular kind of apples) do not restrict
themselves to selling only the wares implied in their
name. Often something is chosen as the basis of the
name which to us nowadays, at any rate, is not the
most important thing: in Danish, *hørkræmmer* (flax
dealer) stands for a man who deals in coal and a
great deal besides, *urtekræmmer* (herb-dealer) for one
who did indeed in old days sell herbs, but who does
not do so now, in the ordinary meaning of the word.
He is a grocer Cp. names like Dan. *kolonialvarer* Germ.

kolonialwaaren (groceries) or Engl. *hardware*. Some names mean really nothing in themselves, like the Eng. *undertaker* or *grocer*, which properly means a 'wholesale dealer' (from 'gross') or the Dan. *apoteker* (druggist) from *apotek* which properly means a store, (in another form the word has become *butik*, Fr. *boutique*, used in a wider and more general sense).

It is a trait of mankind at large to go roundabout ways to denote things for which it is not always easy to find short, precise names representing the concept with complete adequacy. The name therefore is often not a really good one, i. e. is not capable of fulfilling its linguistic task, until its origin, or whatever was the ground or inducement for choosing the name, has passed into oblivion. *Anecdote* meant originally 'unpublished': now thousands of anecdotes have been published many times over, and the meaning of the word has changed. *Gymnastics* comes from the Greek 'gymnos', 'naked', now gymnastics are practised in a special dress. *Sport* in earlier times meant *disport*, from the OFr. *se desporter*, to leave off work, to amuse oneself: the word *sport* is in one way better, that is, more restricted to a single meaning, in languages like French, German and Danish which have borrowed the word from English, than it is in English itself, where it has more of its earlier wide meaning, 'amusement'. *Atlas*, as the name for a collection of maps, takes its origin from an old work which had on its title-page a picture of the giant Atlas bearing the globe on his shoulders. *Irony* comes from the Greek *eirōneia* which means dissimulation, and is derived from *eirōn*, 'one who speaks', i. e. one who only *says*

something without meaning it, therefore 'a hypocrite'.
The French *naïf*, *naïve*, comes from Lat. *nativus*,
from *natus*, and so originally meant native, natural.
One might go on giving examples of round-about ways
of assigning names.

Two opposite principles are at work in the fash-
ioning of names (apart from ordinary derivation of
one word from another). Either we take a word
which implies many qualities and apply it to something which has one, or perhaps a few, of these qualities, as when a proper name like Crœsus is applied
to a man who shares with Crœsus the one quality of
being rich. Or we take a word which suggests one
quality, and apply it to something which has that
quality among many others. A *blackcap* is a bird which
with many other characteristics has a black head:
a *bicycle* has many other characteristics than its two
wheels. But in whichever of these two ways a name
is given, a glance into an etymological dictionary of any
language will show how great a part is played by what
is merely accidental, unforeseen and unforeseeable.
The most important thing about a new name is that
by it one should be able to recognize the thing it denotes. But just as in order to recognize a person we
do not need to see the whole man, both front-face and
in profile, and to hear his voice, but are often content merely to see his head, or even part of his face,
or to hear his voice outside the door, so in the world
of language it is often enough to get a bare hint. We
can supply the rest from previous experience. Often,
indeed, we get no more than can be compared with
he way in which we can recognize a friend by his

knock. How pointless is it then to do as many people do, when it is a question of defining some concept or other such as religion, civilization, education, irony, namely to begin by asking 'what does the word come from'? and to think that some light is thrown thereby on the nature of the thing itself. This is a learned form of superstitious belief in the power of the name, related to the primitive superstition that the name has a magical potency. We get no further at all towards understanding what a tragedy is when we are informed that the word must once have meant 'goat-song', nor in understanding what a comedy is by learning that it means 'festal-song', 'banquet-song', whatever the Greek *kōmos* comes from.

We see 'the universal human element' again in the fact that words of the form *mama, papa, tata, nana* crop up in the most different places as expressions for the concepts which are earliest formed in the consciousness of the child: mother, father, nurse, breast, food.[1] It is likewise natural that there should be great agreement between different languages in all the words in which sound is symbolized by the reproduction of the actual impression made by the sound, and what is connected with it. The vowel *i* is a symbol in many words in all possible languages for what is little, fine, slim, quick, etc.

Common to all mankind again is a fondness for reduplications. There are various kinds of them, from the case in which the whole word is repeated to strengthen the effect ('very, very glad', 'this too too solid flesh') to the many weakened forms, in which

[1] See my *Language* p. 154.

only the first syllable, or a single sound, is duplicated. Under this head come also the everywhere popular, more or less meaningless, words with reduplicating-variations of different sorts, especially with rime or change of vowel, words, that is, like *hurly-burly*, *hugger-mugger* on the one hand, and *zigzag*, *fiddle-faddle*, *shilly-shally*, *nicknacks*, etc., on the other. [1]

In grammar, different languages follow such different courses that it might seem utterly hopeless to try to find anything in this sphere that was common to mankind at large. And yet even here, if we look deep enough, there is something common to all. Delacroix perhaps goes too far when he writes that 'in a certain sense language is everywhere one and the same, and there is only one human language: the differences in languages are only an embroidery on this common canvas' But this is certain that we see everywhere in the history of languages a uniform striving to be quit of the same superfluous distinctions and to reduce the grammatical apparatus to the simplest possible, to a system in which the great inner-syntactical, logical, or rational categories are denoted sharply and unmistakeably. Such distinctions as those between one and more, he and she, between animate and inanimate, between past, present, and future, between the three persons — distinctions which in the infancy of languages were chaotically coupled with one another and with obscure ideas of a quite different kind — come by this means to stand out sharper and sharper, while a logic com-

---

[1] I have myself collected a number of examples of these and similar formations, and Mr. E. Sapir has sent me his own large collections, which I hope some day to be able to work over.

mon to all mankind breaks radiantly through the barriers of linguistic expression. But on this topic I must content myself with these brief suggestions.

The grammatical substratum is, however, not the only thing that the languages of mankind have in common. There is something else which has only become prominent in recent times, because it is an outcome of the historical evolution of a community of culture, brought about chiefly by the increased facilities for human intercourse.

I mean the ever increasing number of words which are common, at least to a great part of the world. First there are the expressions for many of the products of civilization, good and evil — coffee, tea, chocolate, cigar, cigarette, alcohol, opium. Then words like nature, luxury, culture, telegraph, radio, bacteria, comedy, tragedy, act, university, dance, canon, paper — one could go on, though even in these words there are some differences between different languages.

But the number of these words representing a common civilization, combined with the common logical substratum, justify us in working for an international language — not a world-language, standing in a hostile attitude to the existing national languages and intended to supplant them, but an auxiliary language to help out the national languages on all occasions where they come short; that is, in meetings of people who speak different languages by birth and cannot make themselves mutually understood. But if an international language is ever to be realized, it must have a scientific foundation: it must utilize to the fullest extent the results of scientific investigation in regard to those parts of grammar which are really common to all mankind, while it must know how to take the fullest possible advantage of the community in cultural words already attained. The conscientious work done in the last few decads for this end has already brought us so far towards the goal, that an auxiliary language, which will be extremely serviceable both scientifically and practically, is now in sight. Its adoption will be of immeasurable advantage to the whole of humanity. But the subject is too great to be treated here, and I must close.

In the course of these lectures I have repeatedly tried to show that something common to all mankind lies concealed behind the varied multiplicity of phenomena. Common to all, in the main, is the mutual play of individual and community which I have tried to depict. Everywhere we see the same conditions governing the power or the importance of the individual in face of what is conventionally 'correct' in language: everywhere, a movement from small to great linguistic communities: similar political, social, literary and geographical causes, similar conditions of habitation and communication. leading to the development and diffusion of great national languages. The individual's reaction to the norm leads to the invention of slang, which presents similar traits in Paris, London, New York and Copenhagen. In our discussion of taboo we were able to leap- from Greenland to Madagascar and find kindred customs, resting on a common natural foundation: we found that schoolboys in Europe and Maoris in New Zealand took delight in the same kind of concealment-languages, and that religious language and

poetical language had many common features where-
ever on the earth's surface they had sprung up. May
we then not be permitted to say that our languages
with all their diversities disclose the existence of a
great common factor in men s trend of thought and
men's craving for expression?

It is the task of science to collect single facts
and combine them into great wholes in order to discover general laws, and on the other hand to throw
a light from the whole over the otherwise isolated
units in order to explain them. I have striven here,
to the best of my poor ability, to contribute to this
mighty task in one single field, and it has been a
special pleasure to me to be able to do this by the
help of the Norwegian Institute for Comparative Research
in Human Culture, which, by all appearances, is destined
to be of extraordinary service to international science
to the benefit of all mankind.

ABBREVIATIONS OF BOOK TITLES

Bauche = H. Bauche, Le Langage populaire, Paris 1920.

BSL = Bulletin de la Société de Linguistique.

Bücher AR = Karl Bücher, Arbeit und Rhythmus, 2. aufl. Leipzig 1899.

Delacroix LP = H. Delacroix, Le Langage et la Pensée, Paris 1924.

Ellis EEP = A. J. Ellis, Early English Pronunciation, London 1869 ff.

GS = O. Jespersen, Growth and Structure of the English Language. 4th ed. Leipzig 1923.

IF = Indogermanische Forschungen.

Language = O. Jespersen, Language, its Nature, etc. London 1922.

Lévy-Bruhl, FM = L. Lévy-Bruhl, Les Fonctions Mentales dans les sociétés inférieures. Paris 1910.

Litbl. = Literaturblatt f. germ. u. rom. Philologie.

Madvig 1857 = J. N. Madvig, Universitetsprogram, København 1857.

Meillet Gr = A. Meillet, Aperçu d'une Histoire de la Langue Grecque. Paris 1913.

—LH = Linguistique Historique et Linguistique .Générale. Paris 1921.

Meinhof MSA = C. Meinhof, Die moderne Sprachforschung in Afrika, Berlin 1910.

NED = A New English Dictionary, by Murray, etc. Oxford.

Niceforo GA = A. Niceforo, Le Génie de l'Argot, Paris 1912.

Sainéan, LP = L. Sainéan, Le Langage Parisien au XIX ciècle, Paris 1920.

Sayce P = A. H. Sayce, The Principles of Comparative Philology, London 1875.

Streitberg Gesch. = Geschichte der indogerm. Sprachwissenschaft, Strassburg 1916 f.

Vossler FK = K. Vossler, Frankreichs Kultur im Spiegel seiner Sprachentwickelung. Heidelberg 1921.